WOMEN WITH ADHD

The Essential Guide to Overcome the Hidden Struggles of Living with Adult ADHD. Manage Your Symptoms and Live your Best Life

Philip Smith

Table of Contents

INTRODUCTION

Attention Deficit Hyperactivity Disorder (ADHD) is a common disorder, occurring in around 5% of school-age children and 2.5% of adults. People affected by ADHD typically show high levels of symptoms relating to poor concentration, disorganization, impulsivity, hyperactivity, and mood instability.

ADHD produces symptoms characterized by:

- Distractibility
- Hyperactivity
- Poor impulse control
- Forgetfulness

The "attention deficit" component of ADHD refers to inattention or difficulty focusing for long periods and being easily distractible. The "hyperactivity" portion of ADHD is used to describe behaviour that is restless, agitated, and difficult to resist. Hyperactive individuals often appear as if they NEED to move. They are in almost constant motion and frequently make excessive noise.

Although impulsivity is not included in the diagnostic label, it is also considered a behaviour characteristic of this disorder. When impulsivity is paired with hyperactivity, the person appears to act without prior thought or intention. Impulsive behaviours are often intrusive, rude, and dangerous, sometimes resulting in

INTRODUCTION

Attention Deficit Hyperactivity Disorder (ADHD) is a common [illegible]

[illegible]

accidents. For example, children may not think about landing when they jump off a ledge to catch a ball.

Given that all children tend to exhibit some of the characteristics of the behaviour of ADHD, such as daydreaming, restlessness, or thoughtlessness, it is essential to understand the difference between normal behaviours and an actual disorder.

Actual ADHD symptoms are long-term and severe enough to impair someone's everyday functioning. Moreover, symptoms must occur in more than one environment.

For example, in children, the ADHD symptoms interfere with success in school and relationships with parents, siblings, or peers. For adults, ADHD interferes with both work and family functioning.

ADHD was initially thought only to affect some children, but it is now widely recognized that it can continue into adulthood and across a person's lifespan. Research has shown that about two-thirds of children diagnosed with ADHD will continue to live with it as they become adults, potentially causing significant ongoing disability. Diagnosis is not always made in childhood, and, therefore, it is even less likely to be correctly diagnosed in adulthood.

Adults with Attention Deficit Hyperactivity Disorder may have a history of struggling academically, frequent job changes, or an inability to stay in employment at all. Some have more severe than average difficulties in their personal lives, i.e. people with ADHD are twice as likely to be divorced or have relationship issues and are more likely to have been arrested. ADHD is also typically associated with increased road traffic accidents and increased dropout rates from further education.

Although some people with undiagnosed ADHD do cope well and achieve to an exceptional level, this tends to be due to receiving considerable support or putting in effort well above and beyond their peers. Many people diagnosed in later life see that, had they been diagnosed earlier, they could have achieved more.

Adult ADHD is a highly treatable condition. However, it has only recently been understood and recognized by many health care professionals as a condition in its own right; and it is still commonly confused with other mental health disorders or not diagnosed at all.

CHAPTER 1: WHAT IS ADHD

What Is ADHD?

Attention-deficit/hyperactivity disorder (ADHD) is one of the most common mental disorders affecting children. ADHD also affects many adults. Symptoms of ADHD include:

- Inattention (not being able to keep focus)
- Hyperactivity (excess movement that is not fitting to the setting)
- Impulsivity (hasty acts that occur at the moment without thought)

Attention-deficit/hyperactivity disorder (ADHD) is marked by difficulty concentrating, hyperactivity/impulsiveness, disorganization, low frustration tolerance, and other symptoms that impair everyday functioning. Treatment and lifestyle changes can help manage the symptoms so you can live well with ADHD.

A lot of adults do not know that they have attention deficit hyperactivity disorder (ADHD). The symptoms of ADHD can affect adults and children, even among people who did receive a diagnosis when they were young. ADHD is a neurodevelopmental condition that affects a person's behaviour. People with ADHD have difficulty concentrating and are easily distracted.

Many adults with ADHD symptoms do not receive a diagnosis of the condition. This can affect a person's chance of receiving treatment. Without treatment, ADHD can affect their work performance, mental health, and relationships. Keep reading to learn more about the risks of untreated ADHD in adults, as well as the symptoms, causes, and treatment options associated with ADHD. This article also covers when to see a doctor.

ADHD can affect children and adults, but the condition often goes unnoticed in people aged 18–44 years. There are no laboratory tests that diagnose ADHD. When treating symptoms in adults, a doctor may evaluate a person's medical and developmental history and look at their behaviours and how they interact with those around them.

Attention deficit hyperactivity disorder (ADHD) is a neuropsychiatric disorder that makes it difficult to pay attention, control impulsivity (taking action before fully thinking things through), or manage excitable behaviour (the person is squirming/fidgeting or "hyperactive"). The disorder interferes with the quality of life by intruding on day-to-day functioning.

Three different types of ADHD have been identified based on criteria from the American Psychiatric Association. These are:

- Predominantly inattentive presentation.
- Predominantly hyperactive-impulsive presentation.

- Combined presentation (inattentive and hyperactive-impulsive symptoms are present).

Adults who have significant problems with inattention, but exhibit few or no symptoms of hyperactivity, are said to have the predominantly inattentive presentation of ADHD. People with this type of ADHD have trouble paying attention to details, are easily distracted, often have problems organizing or finishing tasks, and often forget routine chores (such as paying bills on time or returning phone calls).

According to one 2020 study, doctors can identify ADHD more quickly in men. This may be because women tend to have different symptoms of ADHD and do not always display the behaviours typically associated with it.

For example, "internalizing" symptoms, such as inattentiveness, are more prominent in women than "externalizing" ones, such as hyperactivity and impulsivity. This means that "a low index of clinical suspicion exists" in this group, which, in turn, means that doctors may be less likely to spot the condition.

The same research also points out that women with ADHD may be more likely to develop better coping mechanisms than men to hide their symptoms. This may lead to misdiagnosis or a lack of treatment.

What Causes Attention Deficit Hyperactivity Disorder (ADHD) In Adults?

The causes of attention deficit hyperactivity disorder (ADHD) are unclear, but the condition often runs in families. There appears to be a genetic and neurobiological basis for ADHD. Usually, adults with the predominantly inattentive form of ADHD first developed it during childhood and adolescence. They were likely reprimanded in elementary or middle school, were consistently distracted, and turned in incomplete work.

However, because children with this form of ADHD usually are not hyperactive, the disorder might have gone unrecognized until they reached adolescence or adulthood. This is especially true for girls and women with inattentive ADHD. Girls may be more quiet and passive than those who do not have the disorder, and therefore they do not stand out in the classroom. At times, adult women can go undiagnosed until one of their children is diagnosed with ADHD. At this point, they might recognize similarities in their behaviour patterns and seek professional help.

Researchers are studying environmental trauma (the personal and social interpretation of trauma and responses to the trauma) and other issues related to pregnancy or early life exposure (environmental toxins, alcohol and tobacco use during pregnancy, premature birth, low birth weight) as other possible factors that may play a role in ADHD.

What Are Symptoms Of Attention Deficit Hyperactivity Disorder (ADHD), Inattentive Type, In Adults?

According to the American Psychiatric Association's diagnostic criteria, there are nine symptoms associated with inattention. Although nearly everyone experiences inattention problems at times, people with the predominantly inattentive presentation of ADHD frequently experience the following symptoms. These symptoms may intrude and interfere in their daily functioning at work, with family members, or in social situations. The nine symptoms associated with the predominantly inattentive presentation of ADHD are:

- Often has trouble staying focused on tasks at work, home, or play
- Frequently does not pay close attention to details or makes careless mistakes at work or while doing other tasks
- Often has trouble organizing tasks or activities (misses deadlines, disorganized work)
- Is easily distracted
- Frequently does not follow through on instructions or fails to complete work assignments, chores, or other activities.
- Often forgets doing routine chores (like paying bills, returning phone calls, keeping appointments)
- Avoids tasks that require extended periods of mental focus (preparing reports, filling out forms)

- Often loses items needed to complete tasks or activities
- She does not appear to be listening even when spoken to directly

Adults May Have A Predominantly Inattentive Presentation Of ADHD If They:

- Experience severe or chronic problems due to five or more of these symptoms
- Have no other mental health disorder that could be the cause of these symptoms
- Have few-to-no symptoms of hyperactivity or impulsivity
- Other psychological conditions, such as depression or anxiety, can also accompany ADHD in adults.

Types Of ADHD

The book explores how ADHD impacts many areas of the brain and the three neurotransmitters: dopamine, serotonin, and Gaba. The affected brain areas are the prefrontal cortex and cerebellum, which control executive functions of concentration, attention span, judgment, organization, planning, and impulse control; the anterior cingulate, which helps the brain shift gears and detect errors; the temporal lobes, which involve memory, learning, emotional reactions, mood stability, and visual processing; the basal ganglia, large structures deep in the brain that help produce the neurotransmitter dopamine; and the limbic system, which sets emotional tone and bonding. Following is a summary of amen's seven types of add along with his proposals for treatment.

1. Classic ADHD

Symptoms: Inattentive, distractible, hyperactive, disorganized, and impulsive. Regular brain activity at rest; decreased brain activity during concentrated tasks.

Cause: Dopamine deficiency; decreased blood flow in the prefrontal cortex and cerebellum and basal ganglia, which helps produce dopamine.

Treatment: Stimulant medications, such as Ritalin, Adderall, Vyvanse, or Concerta, or stimulating supplements, such as Rhodiola, green tea, ginseng, as well as the amino acid l-tyrosine, which is a building block of dopamine; extra physical activity; fish oil that is higher in EPA than in DHA.

2. Inattentive ADHD

Symptoms: Short attention span, distractible, disorganized, procrastinates, may daydream and be introverted; not hyperactive or impulsive; impacts girls as much or more than boys.

Cause: Dopamine deficiency; low activity in the prefrontal cortex.

Treatment: Stimulant medications, such as Adderall, Vyvanse, Concerta, or stimulating supplements, such as amino acid l-tyrosine; high-protein, lower-carbohydrate diet; regular exercise.

3. Over-Focused ADHD

Symptoms: Core symptoms of classic add, trouble shifting attention, going from thought-to-thought or task-to-task, getting stuck in negative thought patterns or behaviours.

Cause: Dopamine and serotonin deficiencies; over-activity in the anterior cingulate gyrus, which makes flexibility difficult.

Treatment: Supplements, such as l-tryptophan, 5-htp (dietary supplement used as an antidepressant), saffron, and inositol (naturally occurring nutrient used to boost alertness, focus, mood, and mental clarity); otherwise antidepressants Effexor, pristine, or Cymbalta; avoid high-protein diet, which may trigger mean behaviour. Neurofeedback.

4. Temporal Lobe ADHD

Symptoms: Core symptoms of classic add, as well as learning, memory, and behavioural problems, such as quick anger, aggression, and mild paranoia.

Cause: Abnormalities in the temporal lobe; decreased activity in the prefrontal cortex.

Treatment: Amino acid Gaba (gamma-aminobutyric acid) to calm neural activity and inhibit nerve cells from over-firing or firing erratically; magnesium to help with anxiety and irritability; anticonvulsant medications to help with mood stability; ginkgo or vinpocetine to help with learning and memory problems.

5. Limbic ADHD

Symptoms: Core symptoms of classic add, as well as chronic low-level sadness (not depression): moodiness, low energy, frequent feelings of helplessness or excessive guilt, and chronic low self-esteem.

Cause: Too much activity in the limbic part of the brain (the mood control centre); decreased prefrontal cortex activity, whether concentrating on a task or at rest.

Treatment: Supplements dl-phenylalanine (dlpa), l-tyrosine, and same (s-adenosyl-methionine); anti-depressants Wellbutrin or imipramine; exercise; fish oil and diet modifications.

6. Ring Of Fire ADHD

Symptoms: Sensitivity to noise, light, touch; periods of mean, nasty behaviour; unpredictable behaviour; speaking fast; anxiety and fearfulness.

Cause: A ring of hyperactivity around the brain (the entire brain is overactive, with too much activity across the cerebral cortex and other areas).

Treatment: Stimulants alone may make symptoms worse. Begin with an elimination diet. If an allergy is suspected, neurotransmitters Gaba and serotonin are boosted through supplements, such as Gaba, 5-hp, and l-tyrosine, and medication, if necessary. For medicines, begin with anticonvulsants and the blood pressure drugs guanfacine and clonidine, which calm overall hyperactivity.

7. Anxious ADHD

Symptoms: Core symptoms of classic add, as well as being anxious and tense, having physical stress symptoms like headaches and stomachaches, predicting the worst, freezing in anxiety-provoking situations, primarily if being judged.

Cause: High activity in basal ganglia (the opposite of most ad types, where there is low activity).

Treatment:

- Promote relaxation and increase dopamine and GABA levels.
- Add stimulants, taken alone, make patients more anxious.
- Begin with a range of "calming" supplements, such as l-theanine, relora, magnesium, and holy basil tricyclic antidepressants imipramine or desipramine to lower anxiety, depending on the individual.

Neurofeedback decrease symptoms of anxiety, significantly calm the prefrontal cortex.

CHAPTER 2: ADHD IN WOMEN

ADHD In Women

Women often live with undiagnosed attention-deficit/hyperactivity disorder (ADHD). This happens partly because it's a condition that was traditionally thought to affect primarily men but also because women tend to have less obvious or socially disruptive symptoms than men.

Why ADHD Symptoms In Women Are Often Explained Away

ADHD symptoms in girls are often explained as character traits rather than ADHD. For example, who might think of a girl as spacey, a daydreamer, forgetful, or chatty. Later in life, a woman might reach out for help for her ADHD, only to be diagnosed with depression or anxiety instead.

The good news is that there is an increasing awareness about ADHD symptoms in women, which means women can get the help they need. Women with ADHD face the same feelings of being overwhelmed and exhausted that men with ADHD may feel.

Psychological distress, feelings of inadequacy, low self-esteem, and chronic stress are common. Often women with ADHD feel that their lives are out of control or in chaos, and daily tasks may seem impossibly huge.

Though many women are expected to be caretakers, this role can be challenging for a woman with ADHD. When things feel out of control and trouble organizing and planning her own life, taking care of others seems nearly impossible. This role also may significantly increase her feelings of inadequacy.

How Symptoms Differ In Women

One of the reasons why ADHD often goes undiagnosed in women and girls is that the symptoms often differ from those of men and boys. ADHD comes in three presentations: inattentive, hyperactive/impulsive, and a combination of the two.

Men and boys tend to have the hyperactive/impulsive kind, which may cause them to be fidgety, always on the go, disruptive, restless, talkative, impulsive, impatient, and have mood swings.

Women tend to exhibit the inattentive type, making it hard to focus, pay attention to details, stay organized, listen, and remember things. Some of the characteristics of this type, such as being shy or impulsive, are often viewed as personality traits instead of symptoms.

Studies generally show that while men and women with ADHD are more alike than different, there are a few minor differences. During adolescence, girls tend to have fewer coping strategies and worse self-efficacy than boys. Girls and women have fewer externalizing symptoms such as aggression than men but higher levels of depression and anxiety.

Why ADHD Symptoms In Women Are Often Explained Away

ADHD symptoms in girls are often explained as character traits rather than ADHD. For example, who might think of a girl as spacey, a daydreamer, forgetful, or chatty. Later in life, a woman might reach out for help for her ADHD, only to be diagnosed with depression or anxiety instead.

The good news is that there is an increasing awareness about ADHD symptoms in women, which means women can get the help they need.

Women with ADHD face the same feelings of being overwhelmed and exhausted that men with ADHD may feel.

Psychological distress, feelings of inadequacy, low self-esteem, and chronic stress are common. Often women with ADHD feel that their lives are out of control or in chaos, and daily tasks may seem impossibly huge.

Though many women are expected to be caretakers, this role can be challenging for a woman with ADHD. When things feel out of control and trouble organizing and planning her own life, taking care of others seems nearly impossible. This role also may significantly increase her feelings of inadequacy.

Common Signs Of ADHD In Women

You may notice signs of ADHD in many different areas of your life. Some of these symptoms may be worse or more noticeable in specific contexts, such as at work or school. You may find that you spend a lot of time and effort to look "normal," and hope no one notices the real you.

1. **Relationships**

You wish you could be a better friend, partner, or mom and that you would do the things that other people do. For example, you wish you could remember birthdays, bake cookies, and arrive on time for a date. Because you cannot do the things that society expects women to do, people may think you don't care.

2. **Social Life**

Growing up, you were always described as a tomboy because you had so much energy and liked to be busy. As an adult, friendships can be challenging to navigate because social rules seem complicated. People often say that you talk more than anyone else they know.

While you may be talkative, you dislike going to parties and other social gatherings because they make you feel overwhelmed and shy. Your mind drifts during conversations unless you're the one talking or it's a topic you find very interesting.

3. Work

Being at the office feels difficult. The noise and people make it hard to get work done. You often stay late at the office, as the only time you can work well is when everyone else has left, and it's quiet. Your desk at work is piled high with papers. Even when you make a significant effort to tidy it, it only stays clear for a day or two.

4. School

In school, ADHD symptoms in girls may get overlooked because women are more likely to have inattentive ADHD, which doesn't have the visible behaviour problems that hyperactive/impulsive ADHD usually does. Girls with ADHD may also hyperfocus on things that interest them, which may lead teachers and parents to overlook the possibility of ADHD.

As an adult, you feel frustrated that people you went to school with the pass you by with their achievements, even though you know you're just as bright.

5. Daily Life

It often feels like each day is spent responding to requests and limiting disasters rather than moving forward with your goals. You feel crushing sadness and frustration that you haven't met your potential. Other daily struggles may include:

Paper Clutter: It often feels like you're drowning in paper. At work, home, in your car, and even in your purse. You have an uneasy feeling that unpaid bills and forgotten projects are hiding under the paper. You don't feel organized with money and are usually behind with accounts.

Overspending: You often overspend to compensate for other problems. For example, you don't have a clean outfit to wear for an office party, so you buy a new one. Or you forgot someone's birthday, so you buy an expensive present to make up for it. Shopping trips make you feel better in the moment, but you think regretful later when the credit card bill arrives.

Disorganization: You also spend a lot of time, money, and research on products to help you be more organized, but then you don't use them. You feel very embarrassed to have guests visit your home because it's so cluttered and disorganized.

Indecision: Grocery stores overwhelm you, and you find it hard to decide what to buy.

- You often forget a crucial ingredient for a meal even though you take longer in the store than most people do.
- Relaxing is often tricky. Little things can push you over the top, and you become emotional.
- Many women are relieved to learn that behaviours they have been struggling with for so long are because of ADHD.

Co-Occurring Conditions

Other conditions can also be present, along with ADHD. When you have more than one condition, they are called comorbid conditions or coexisting conditions. Here are some conditions that women often have in addition to their ADHD:

- Substance use disorders, such as alcohol or drugs
- Anxiety disorders, such as social anxiety disorder (SAD) or obsessive-compulsive disorder (OCD)
- Sleep disorders
- Eating disorders, such as anorexia or bulimia
- Mood disorders, like depression or bipolar disorder

It's good to be aware of these coexisting conditions because they can cause symptoms that look similar to ADHD. This, in turn, can make diagnosing ADHD more complex. However, an experienced clinician will be aware of this challenge.

Tips For Women With ADHD

Many women feel a tremendous sense of relief when they find out they have attention deficit hyperactivity disorder (ADHD). For years, they may have blamed themselves for their shortcomings, and their self-esteem has taken a hit. Constantly worrying about every detail of their lives may have led to emotional, mental, and physical exhaustion.

After being diagnosed with ADHD, they finally have an answer, and they know that their symptoms are not their fault. When they realize they have ADHD, feelings of inadequacy can begin to fade away, putting them in a better position to treat and manage their symptoms.

Diagnosing ADHD In Women

Most people have a misperception that ADHD is a disorder for hyperactive schoolboys. Because the way ADHD manifests in women does not fit this stereotype, women often don't get diagnosed until adulthood. A 2014 review of ADHD in women and girls found several obstacles to identifying ADHD in women, including:

Symptoms Presentation: Women tend to internalize symptoms much more than men. Specifically, girls' symptoms veer more toward inattentiveness and disorganization. Families and peers often overlook these symptoms and are therefore less likely to refer them for diagnosis.

Comorbid Psychiatric Disorders: Because ADHD symptoms are generally less disruptive in females, mood disorders (like anxiety or depression) are commonly diagnosed long before they get evaluated for ADHD.

Coping Strategies: Women who develop better-coping strategies than their male counterparts may be able to mask the adverse effects of their ADHD symptoms. For example, many overcompensate with list-making to help them stay organized. Although doing this works, it also makes it very easy for doctors to miss the diagnosis.

For women, issues related to ADHD may worsen into adulthood. For example, after graduating from high school, when the structure of the school is no longer in place, and the academic or workplace standard is more elevated, ADHD symptoms can start to cause more problems.

Hyperactivity In Women

Women can be diagnosed with hyperactivity-impulsivity ADHD, although less frequently than women with inattentive ADHD. Having hyperactivity poses its challenges. You might find you have more physical energy than your peers and be accused of talking constantly. Because you seemed different, you might have memories of feeling rejected, judged, and excluded by your peers. This experience can continue into adulthood.

Tips For Living With ADHD

You can do many things to make it easier to cope with the symptoms of ADHD.

Get Diagnosed

If you think you may have ADHD but haven't officially been diagnosed yet, make this your priority. Getting diagnosed can have a positive effect on how you feel about yourself.

One study found that women could forgive themselves for mistakes in the past and felt more in control of their current lives once they were diagnosed with ADHD. Knowing they weren't crazy and that there was a name for what they were going through provided an enormous sense of relief.

How It Feels To Be Newly Diagnosed

Many people are surprised by the intense emotions they feel when they are diagnosed with ADHD.

Common Emotions Include:

Relief: When you first get an ADHD diagnosis, you may feel happy to have a name that describes what you're experiencing. It may feel validating to know that your symptoms stem from a diagnosed condition.

Anger: After the relief has faded, you may feel angry. Perhaps you don't want ADHD, or maybe you're feeling frustration toward parents or teachers who blamed you for your symptoms.

Sadness: You may feel sad that you didn't get diagnosed earlier, or you may grieve for what your life might have been like if you didn't have ADHD. You may also feel sad for your younger self, who struggled with school and life with undiagnosed ADHD.

What You Can Do

Reassure yourself that all these emotions are normal, even if they are painful at the time. Talk to other people about how you're feeling and be willing to ask for help.

Find an ADHD support group in your area. Meeting other people who have been through a similar experience is constructive. Consider working with a therapist who is knowledgeable about ADHD.

Identify Coexisting Conditions

ADHD rarely travels alone, which means you might have one or more other conditions in addition to your ADHD. Try not to feel alarmed. Knowing what other requirements you have, if any, allows you to treat each one directly, which in turn means you can be your healthiest.

Sometimes symptoms of one condition can be masked by symptoms of ADHD or vice versa. The majority of adults with

ADHD have at least one diagnosed or undiagnosed coexisting psychiatric disorder, including:

- Anxiety disorders
- Bipolar disorder
- Depression
- Personality disorders
- Substance use disorders

This is why it's important to share all your symptoms and concerns with your doctor. Being honest about what you are experiencing doesn't mean that you are complaining. Your doctor needs to know how you feel and what you're struggling with, so they can provide you with the most appropriate treatment.

Drive Safely

Inattention and distractibility are the most common reasons for transport accidents. They are also the most common symptoms experienced by women with ADHD.

Drivers affected by ADHD can increase their safety on the road by doing the following:

- **Drive With A Manual Transmission:** Consider driving a car with a manual gearbox rather than automatic because it forces you to be more engaged in the moment and less likely to zone out.

- **Reduce Distractions:** Before you start to drive, switch your phone off to be distracted by incoming calls or texts. Don't talk on the phone even with a headset.
- **Don't Drink And Drive:** Never drink and go or take recreational drugs, as these can further reduce your attention.

Let Go Of Perfectionism

Let go of the need to be perfect. Spending too much time on small things that don't significantly impact your life to the detriment of more essential tasks creates undue stress and anxiety.

For example, you might spend hours finding the perfect font for a report for work while neglecting to start a due tomorrow presentation. Instead of putting pressure on yourself to meet impossibly high standards, work on putting things into perspective.

Manage Your Time

Difficulty with time management is common for adult women with ADHD. You may lose track of time, have difficulty following through on plans, or underestimate how much time is needed for a task. You may also spend so much time on a mission known as hyperfocus that nothing else gets done. These difficulties can leave you feeling overwhelmed, frustrated, and exhausted. Below are some tips to help you manage your time better:

1. Get Organized: Whether you have to go to work, run errands, or tackle household chores, it can be helpful to write down your top priorities. Try creating a schedule the night before so that you can start your day strong. Having a "game plan" will help you feel calmer.

2. Identify Your Strengths And Weaknesses: Many women with ADHD say that it takes them longer to do things than other people. Begin by recognizing what you seem to do faster than other people and what makes you more time. When you can take a balanced look at your strengths and weaknesses, it will help your confidence and self-esteem.

3. Allow Yourself Extra Time: Make sure you have plenty of time to finish a project by giving yourself some cushion. Get in the habit of giving yourself an additional 10 minutes for every 30 minutes you think it will take you to complete a task.

4. Use Timers: Allot yourself a limited amount of time for each task and use a timer to alert you when your time is up. The timer gives you an audible signal to stop what you are working on not to lose track of time.

Exercise

If you have hyperactivity, try incorporating physical activity into your daily routine. Not only will it help you feel focused and calm, but exercise is great for your physical and mental health. You can channel your energy in many positive ways. Take this opportunity to become active in your community, help a loved one, or find a project that fulfils you. You may even discover a new hobby.

Risks Of Untreated ADHD In Adults

ADHD can have a significant impact on adults if they do not receive treatment for the condition. It can also affect people living with them.

Some of the risks associated with untreated ADHD in adults include:

1. Low Self-Esteem, Depression, And Anxiety: Women are more likely to have low self-esteem if they have ADHD. They are also more likely to experience significant psychological distress such as severe anxiety and depression. Chronic stress due to these issues can also lead to other conditions, such as fibromyalgia.

2. Difficulty In Relationships: We found that the spouses of people with ADHD may feel more neglected than those living with individuals without ADHD symptoms. However, it is also important to note that the study used self-report questionnaires instead of looking at anyone's medical history of ADHD.

3. Job Instability: A systematic review of multiple studies found that untreated ADHD in adults can lead to job instability. People with ADHD may be less likely to graduate from college or high school and may, therefore, find it more challenging to have a stable income compared with those without ADHD. This supports this idea, suggesting that adults with ADHD may be unable to stay focused at work, leading to difficulty holding down a job for an extended period.

4. Negative Parent-Child Interactions: Untreated ADHD in adults can cause conflicts in a parent-child relationship. Parents with ADHD may have more difficulty controlling their emotions and impulses, leading to frustration and conflict with children.

5. Drug And Alcohol Misuse: It also links the symptoms of ADHD with a higher likelihood of misusing psychoactive substances, misusing alcohol, and being more susceptible to nicotine addiction.

6. Increased Mortality Rate: ADHD with a significantly higher mortality rate. The mortality rate ratio was even higher in those who received an ADHD diagnosis in adulthood than people who received a correct ADHD diagnosis in childhood.

CHAPTER 3: ADHD AND RELATIONSHIPS

The distractibility, disorganization, and impulsivity characteristic of adults (ADHD) can negatively impact multiple areas of life, but the symptoms associated with ADHD can be particularly troubling for relationships. When one or both partners struggle with ADHD, intimate relationships can be damaged by misunderstandings, frustration, and resentment. The good news is that learning about how your ADHD affects the relationship can help you find strategies and tools to improve communication with your partner and develop a healthier, happier relationship as a result.

Understanding The Symptoms Of Adult ADHD

The defining feature of ADHD is a persistent pattern of inattention and hyperactivity-impulsivity that interfere with functioning (in more than one area) for at least six months. For adults, hyperactivity often manifests as restlessness or wearing others down.

- Failure to pay close attention to details
- Difficulty remembering information
- Difficulty following directions
- Difficulty concentrating or remaining on task
- Struggles to organize tasks
- Problem completing work on time

- Chronic lateness and forgetfulness
- Social intrusiveness – frequent interruptions
- Hyper-focus: Intense focus on things of interest (i.e. shopping online, video games)
- Poor planning
- Easily stressed out
- Explosive temper
- Difficulty sitting still
- Excessive talking
- Easily bored

Symptoms Of Adult ADHD That Interfere With Relationships

The biggest challenge to making the necessary changes to improve your relationship is understanding the signs that have the most significant impact on your partner. Once you know how your symptoms influence your behaviour with your partner, you can learn how to manage them.

Adult ADHD can be tricky because symptoms vary from person to person. These specific symptoms can impact how you relate to your partner:

Inattention: Adults with ADHD can lose focus during conversations, which leaves the partner feeling devalued. Inattention can also lead to mindlessly agreeing to things that you later forget. This can be frustrating and lead to resentment.

Forgetfulness: Even when adults with ADHD are paying attention, they might still forget what was discussed. This can cause others to see the person as unreliable or incapable.

Impulsivity: This symptom of adult ADHD can lead to frequent interruptions during conversations or blurting out thoughts without considering the feelings of others. This can result in hurt feelings.

Disorganization: Difficulty organizing and completing tasks can lead to household chaos. This can cause resentment and frustration for the partner, who might feel like they do more work at home.

Explosive Temper: Many adults with ADHD have difficulty regulating their emotions. This can result in angry outbursts that leave partners feeling hurt or fearful.

While the adult with ADHD in the relationship is at risk of feeling micromanaged and overwhelmed with criticism, the non-ADHD partner might feel disconnected, lonely, or underappreciated. It's essential to focus on how the ADHD symptoms impact the relationship instead of blaming one another for a breakdown in the bond.

Possible Benefits Of ADHD In Relationships

Some traits that are common in people with ADHD may be beneficial in relationships. Highlighting the following characteristics:

Positivity: People with ADHD tend to have a positive outlook, which can help navigate the difficulties of any relationship.

Sociability: People with ADHD are often talkative and friendly, and participants in the study said that this helped them form and strengthen relationships.

Openness: People with ADHD tend to be open, and so they may be happy to speak about topics that others may avoid or ignore.

Empathy: People with ADHD may be more willing to help and see things from other people's points of view.

Resilience: Actively working to overcome the challenges of ADHD tends to make a person more resilient. In the context of a relationship, a person with ADHD may persist when others give up or have different coping skills.

The Attention Deficit Disorder Association emphasizes that people with ADHD can have lasting, loving relationships.

Adult ADHD And Relationships

Attention deficit hyperactivity disorder, can cause misunderstandings, frustrations, and resentments in your closest relationships. But there are ways to build a healthier, happier partnership.

How Does ADHD Or ADD Affect Relationships?

While the distractibility, disorganization, and impulsivity of attention deficit hyperactivity disorder (ADHD or ADD) can cause problems in many areas of adult life, these symptoms can be particularly damaging when it comes to your closest relationships. This is especially true if the symptoms of ADHD have never been properly diagnosed or treated.

If you're the person with ADHD, you may feel like you're constantly being criticized, nagged, and micromanaged. No matter what you do, nothing seems to please your spouse or partner. You don't feel respected as an adult, so you find yourself avoiding your partner or saying whatever you have to get them off your back. You wish your significant other could relax even a little bit and stop trying to control every aspect of your life. You wonder what happened to the person you fell in love with.

If you're in a relationship with someone who has ADHD, you may feel lonely, ignored, and unappreciated. You're tired of taking care of everything on your own and being the only responsible party in the relationship. You don't feel like you can rely on your partner. They never seem to follow through on promises, and you're forced to constantly issue reminders and demands or else just do things yourself. Sometimes it feels as if your significant other just doesn't care.

It's easy to see how the feelings on both sides can contribute to a destructive cycle in the relationship. The non-ADHD partner complains, nags, and becomes increasingly resentful, while the ADHD partner, feeling judged and misunderstood, gets defensive and pulls away. In the end, nobody is happy. But it doesn't have to be this way.

You can build a healthier, more delighted partnership by learning about the role ADHD plays in your relationship and how both of you can choose more positive and productive ways to respond to challenges and communicate with each other. With these strategies, you can add greater understanding to your relationship and bring you closer together.

Put Yourself In Your Partner's Shoes

The first step in turning your relationship around is learning to see things from your partner's perspective. If you've been together a long time or you've had the same fights again and again, you might think that you already understand where your partner is coming from. But don't underestimate how easy it is to misinterpret your partner's actions and intentions. You and your partner are more different than you think, especially if only one of you has ADHD. And just because you've heard it all before doesn't mean you've indeed taken in what your partner is saying.

When emotions are running high, as they usually do around ADHD relationship issues, it's complicated to maintain objectivity and perspective.

The best way to put yourself in your partner's shoes is to ask and then simply listen. Find a time to sit down and talk when you're not already upset. Let your partner describe how they feel without interruption from you to explain or defend yourself. When your partner is finished, repeat back the main points you've heard them say, and ask if you understood correctly. You may want to write the ends down so you can reflect on them later. When your partner is finished, it's your turn. Ask them to do the same for you and listen with fresh ears and an open mind.

Tips For Increasing Understanding In Your Relationship

Study up on ADHD. The more both of you learn about ADHD and its symptoms, the easier it will be to see how it influences your relationship. You may find that a light bulb comes on. So many of your issues as a couple finally make sense! Remembering that an ADHD brain is hardwired differently than a brain without ADHD can help the non-ADHD partner take symptoms less personally. For the partner with ADHD, it can be a relief to understand what's behind some of your behaviours and know that you can take steps to manage your symptoms.

Acknowledge the impact your behaviour has on your partner. If you're the one with ADHD, it's essential to recognize how your untreated symptoms affect your partner. If you're the non-ADHD partner, consider how your nagging and criticism makes your spouse feel. Don't dismiss your partner's complaints or disregard them because you don't like how they bring them up or react to you.

Separate who your partner is from their symptoms or behaviours. Instead of labelling your partner "irresponsible," recognize their forgetfulness and lack of follow-through as symptoms of ADHD. Remember, symptoms aren't character traits. The same goes for the non-ADHD partner too. Recognize that nagging usually arises from feelings of frustration and stress, not because your partner is an unsympathetic harpy.

ADHD Often Feels:

Take Responsibility For Your Role

Once you've put yourself in your partner's shoes, it's time to accept responsibility for your role in the relationship. Progress starts once you become aware of your contributions to the problems you have as a couple. This goes for the non-ADHD partner as well.

While the ADHD partner's symptoms may trigger an issue, the symptoms alone aren't to blame for the relationship problem. The non-ADHD partner response to the bothersome symptom can either open the door for cooperation, compromise or provoke misunderstandings and hurt feelings. If you're the one with ADHD, you're also responsible for the way you react to your partner's concerns. Your reaction can either make your significant other feel validated and heard or disregarded and ignored.

Break Free Of The Parent-Child Dynamic

Many couples feel stuck in an unsatisfying parent-child relationship, with the non-ADHD partner in the role of the parent and the partner with ADHD in the part of the child. It often starts when the partner with ADHD fails to follow through on tasks, such as forgetting to pay the cable bill, leaving clean laundry in a pile on the bed, or leaving the kids stranded after promising to pick them up. The non-ADHD partner takes on more and more of the household responsibilities.

The more lopsided the partnership becomes, the more resentful they feel. It becomes harder to appreciate the ADHD spouse's positive qualities and contributions. Of course, the partner with ADHD senses this. They start to feel like there's no point in even trying and dismisses the non-ADHD spouse as controlling and impossible to please. So what can you do to break this pattern?

Tips For The Non-ADHD Partner:

- You can't control your spouse, but you can manage your actions. Put an immediate stop to verbal attacks and nagging. Neither gets results.
- Encourage your partner when they make progress and acknowledge achievements and efforts.
- When possible, try to focus on your partner's intentions rather than what they do. They may lose concentration when listening to you, for example, but that doesn't mean they don't care about what you have to say.
- Stop trying to "parent" your partner. It is destructive to your relationship and demotivating to your spouse.

Tips For The Partner With ADHD:

- Acknowledge the fact that your ADHD symptoms are interfering with your relationship. It's not just a case of your partner being unreasonable.
- Explore treatment options. As you learn to manage your symptoms and become more reliable, your partner will ease off.
- If solid emotions derail conversations with your partner, agree in advance that you need to take a time out to calm down and refocus before continuing.
- Find ways to spoil your spouse. If your partner feels cared for by you even in small ways, they will feel less like your parent.

Stop Fighting And Start Communicating

As you've already seen, communication often breaks down between partners when ADHD is in the mix. One partner feels overburdened. The other feels attacked. They end up fighting each other rather than tackling the issue.

To Improve Communication:

- Do what you can to defuse emotional volatility. If need be, take time to cool off before discussing an issue.
- When you have the conversation, listen closely to your partner.
- Ask yourself what you're arguing about.

1. Don't Bottle Up Your Emotions: Fess up to your feelings, no matter how ugly. Get them out in the open, where you can work through them as a couple.

2. You're Not A Mind Reader: Don't make assumptions about your partner's motivations. Avoid the "if my spouse loved me..." trap. If your partner does something that upsets you, address it directly rather than silently stewing.

3. Watch What You Say And How You Say It: Avoid critical words and questions that put your partner on the defensive ("Why can't you ever do what you said you would?" or "How many times do I have to tell you?").

4. Find The Humour In The Situation: Learn to laugh over the inevitable miscommunications and misunderstandings. Laughter relieves tension and brings you closer together.

Improving Your Communication Skills When You Have ADHD

ADHD symptoms can interfere with communication. The following tips can help you have more satisfying conversations with your partner and other people.

1. Communicate Face To Face Whenever Possible: Nonverbal cues such as eye contact, tone of voice, and gestures communicate much more than words alone. To understand the emotion behind the comments, you need to share with your partner in person rather than via phone, text, or email.

2. Listen Actively And Don't Interrupt: While the other person is talking, make an effort to maintain eye contact. If you find your mind wandering, mentally repeat their words, so you follow the conversation. Make an effort to avoid interrupting.

3. Ask Questions: Instead of launching into whatever is on your mind or the many things on your mind, ask the other person a question. It will let them know you're paying attention.

4. Request A Repeat: If your attention wanders, tell the other person as soon as you realize it and ask them to repeat what was just said. If you let the conversation go too long when your mind is elsewhere, it will only get tougher to reconnect.

5. Manage Your Emotions: If you're unable to discuss certain subjects without flying off the handle or saying things you later regret, consider practising mindfulness meditation. As well as helping to lower impulsivity and improve focus, regular mindfulness meditation can offer you greater control over your emotions and prevent the emotional outbursts that can be so damaging to a relationship.

Work Together As A Team

Just because one partner has ADHD doesn't mean you can't have a balanced, mutually fulfilling relationship. The key is to learn to work together as a team. A healthy relationship involves give and take, with both participating fully in the partnership and looking for ways to support each other.

Take some time on both sides to identify what you're good at and which tasks are most challenging for you. If your spouse is vital in an area in which you're weak, perhaps they can take over that responsibility, and vice versa. It should feel like an equal exchange. If you're both weak in a particular area, brainstorm how to get outside help. For example, if neither of you is good with money, you could hire a bookkeeper or research money management apps that make budgeting easier.

1. Divide Tasks And Stick To Them: The non-ADHD partner may be more suited to handling the bills and doing the errands while managing the children and cooking.

2. Schedule Weekly Sit-Downs: Meet once a week to address issues and assess the progress you've made as a couple.

3. Evaluate The Division Of Labour: Make a list of chores and responsibilities and rebalance the workload if either one of you is shouldering the bulk of the load.

4. Delegate, Outsource And Automate: You and your partner don't have to do everything yourselves. If you have children, assign them chores. You might also consider hiring a cleaning service, signing up for grocery delivery, or setting up automatic bill payments.

5. Split Up Individual Tasks, If Necessary: If the partner with ADHD has trouble completing tasks, the non-ADHD partner may need to step in as the "closer." Account for this in your arrangement to avoid resentments.

Work On Communication Skills

Communication often breaks down when one partner has ADHD. More often than not, the behaviours on the surface (i.e. she's always late for dinner) mask a more profound issue (he feels underappreciated because she never shows up on time.)

Couples also tend to fall into a "parent-child" dynamic, where the non-ADHD partner feels responsible for everything, and the ADHD partner feels like a child. This chronic pattern of micromanaging and underachievement can result in feelings of shame and insecurity for the ADHD partner.

When couples work to improve communication skills, they can restore balance to the relationship. Try these strategies to communicate effectively with your partner:

- Use "I feel" statements to focus on feelings and avoid blame
- Communicate face-to-face as often as possible – nonverbal cues are important
- Repeat and rephrase – to avoid allowing your mind to wander, repeat what your partner says and rephrase for clarification
- Ask questions
- Text yourself essential takeaways from the conversation (especially if your partner asks you to assist with specific tasks)
- Talk about how your symptoms impair your ability to remember things or follow through on tasks. Sharing your struggles helps your partner understand how ADHD impacts your behaviour
- Hold eye contact when listening.

- For extended conversations, consider a fidget toy like a squeeze ball to keep your mind engaged.
- **Focus On Teamwork:** To create balance in a relationship, two partners have to work together. Having ADHD doesn't mean that you can't find balance; it means that you have to rely on open and honest communication and feedback to find ways to help one another.
- **Divide Tasks Based On Strengths:** If ADHD interferes with your ability to pay bills on time or manage money, ask your partner to handle that task. When couples divide tasks based on their strengths, they get through their to-do lists without either partner feeling overburdened or resentful.
- **Evaluate The Workload:** Have a weekly meeting at a predetermined time to discuss the workload and rebalance the tasks if you feel overwhelmed. Weekly check-in gives you the chance to consider how you're doing with your household tasks and whether or not you need a change. Weekly check-ins are also an excellent opportunity to slow down and connect and plan time together to strengthen your bond. When one partner has ADHD, relationships can quickly become overwhelmed by the focus to attend to tasks together to reduce frustration. Still, it's just as important to spend time together enjoying each other's company.

- **Delegate Tasks:** You and your partner don't have to manage every aspect of the household independently (mainly if failure to complete tasks is a common problem impacting your relationship.) If you have children, assign age-appropriate chores to help keep the house organized. Automatic bill pay can be beneficial for adults with ADHD. If you can afford it, you might also consider a monthly cleaning service.
- **Rely On Routines:** Routines, schedules, and visual planners (think wall-size whiteboard calendar) help adults with ADHD know what to expect, stay on task, and complete essential duties. When couples coping with ADHD use organizational systems to take some of the guesswork out of the daily grind, they can focus more on connection than completing tasks and chores.

Create A Practical Plan

If you have ADHD, you probably aren't very good at organizing or setting up systems. But that doesn't mean you aren't able to follow a plan once it's in place. This is an area where the non-ADHD partner can provide invaluable assistance. They can help you set up a system and routine you can rely on to help you stay on top of your responsibilities.

Start by analyzing the most frequent things you fight about, such as chores or chronic lateness. Then think about practical things you can do to solve them. It might be an extensive wall calendar with checkboxes next to each person's daily tasks for forgotten chores. For chronic lateness, you might set up a calendar on your smartphone, complete with timers to remind you of upcoming events.

Your ADHD Relationship Survival Guide

1. You, Me, And ADHD: Attention deficit hyperactivity disorder can send your most important relationship off the rails. Distraction, procrastination, and other ADHD symptoms can stir anger, frustration, and hurt feelings for both the person with ADHD and the partner. But your marriage or relationship can thrive with proper treatment and tactics to ward off misunderstandings.

2. Distraction: This is the main symptom of ADHD. Your ADHD partner doesn't seem to listen when you talk or fails to follow through on promises. You feel unheard, ignored, and unwanted. In reality, they may love you very much but are too distracted by the TV, the phone, or their thoughts to show it.

3. Distraction Strategies: First, calmly tell your ADHD partner how you feel. Bottled-up feelings can lead to resentment and anger. If conversations are a big problem, set a time to talk to your partner face-to-face, away from distractions. It may help to touch your partner while you chat. If you're the one with ADHD and start to zone out, fess up. Ask your partner to repeat what they said. If the conversation goes on too long and your mind wanders, it's harder to reconnect.

4. Hyperfocus: This is the flip side of distraction. You may be so engrossed in something it's hard to shift your attention away. You can't drag yourself away from that new bestseller or look up from your smartphone. Hyperfocus can be a gift for productivity. But unchecked, it can make your loved one feel less important than whatever has grabbed your attention.

5. Hyperfocus Strategies: If you're prone to hyperfocus during certain activities, like online games or crossword puzzles, avoid them close to mealtimes or whenever you need to engage with your partner. Set alarms and track the time you spend on doing one thing. Get up or move to break your preoccupation when you realize you're hyper-focusing. If you're the partner or the spouse, try not to take it personally.

6. Forgetfulness: You blanked out on your dinner date and left your husband stranded at the restaurant. Maybe your power got shut off because you forgot to pay your electric bill. Your partner feels they can't trust you with even basic tasks. You feel like a failure. Anger builds on both sides.

7. Forgetfulness Strategies: Forgetfulness and other ADHD symptoms aren't character flaws. Avoid lectures and don't label the behaviour as rude or uncaring. Don't take over for your partner, either. That can leave you both resentful. Instead, work with your partner to help them remember. Use a day planner or reminders on a smartphone or a laptop.

8. Disorganization: The partner with ADHD may skip chores or leave jobs unfinished. Or constantly misplace the car keys or lose essential papers. Disorganization can cause stress and wasted time and money. It also can lead to nagging and leave the other person feeling controlled.

9. Disorganization Strategies: Calm down and talk about the issues. Then look for fixes. Maybe the partner with ADHD can take charge of cooking and laundry instead of paying bills or organizing carpools. Play to each of your strengths to avoid the chore wars. Respect the ADHD partner's need to keep items in certain spots -- it may be their way of staying organized.

10. Impulsivity: People who have the hyperactive type of ADHD also tend to be impulsive. They often act before thinking. One common problem is impulsive spending. You may blow money on things you don't need or max out the credit cards. Some people may have risky sex or drive dangerously. Or they may blurt out inappropriate comments at parties.

11. Impulsivity Strategies: Who can learn self-control. You can help your partner role-play how to act in social situations. Or how to wait their turn. If you're apt to overspend, bring cash and stick to your shopping list. Cut out temptations. Toss catalogues and unsubscribe from retailers' emails. If impulsive behaviours are out of hand, you may need help from a therapist with expertise in ADHD.

12. Procrastination: We all put off tedious or complex tasks from time to time. But for some people with ADHD, procrastination is a giant hurdle. You might not know how to get started or feel overwhelmed by a project. You may need last-minute deadlines as motivation. That's a recipe for a chaotic lifestyle that's hard on you and your partner.

13. Procrastination Strategies: It's easier to tackle a project when you break it into small chunks. Focus on only the first part -don't think about the rest of it until you finish step one. If you're the partner, see if you can share a part of the task to offer a company. But take care not to take over their responsibility. Most importantly, don't think of procrastination as a personal defect but as a trait to manage.

14. Mood Swings: People with ADHD often have trouble controlling emotions. You might lash out in anger or have sudden or wide mood swings. That's because you feel anxiety and frustration as well as joy and happiness more intensely than some others. That can leave your partner on edge.

15. Mood Swing Strategies: A healthy diet, good sleep, and regular exercise can head off mood swings. Yoga or tai chi can ease stress and help you control your impulses. If you're the partner, don't overreact to flare-ups. Instead, empathize but also explain how they affect you. Go on a hike or do something together.

CHAPTER 4: ADHD AND MOTIVATION

The Mystery Of ADHD Motivation, Solved

Despite the many differences among children and adults with attention deficit disorder (ADHD or ADD), there is one similarity shared by virtually all of them. Although they have considerable chronic difficulty in getting organized and getting started on many tasks, focusing their attention, sustaining their efforts, and utilizing their short-term working memory, all of those diagnosed with ADHD tend to have at least a few specific activities or tasks for which they have no difficulty in exercising these very same functions in a normal or an extraordinary way.

The inconsistency in motivation and performance is the most puzzling aspect of ADHD. It seems like the child or adult with the disorder who can show substantial cause and focus very well for some tasks should do the same for most other jobs that they recognize as important. It appears as if this is a simple problem of lacking "willpower." If you can do it for this, why can't you do the same for that, which is even more important? However, ADHD is not a matter of willpower. It is a problem with the dynamics of the chemistry of the brain.

One Of My Patients Once Told Me: "I've got a sexual metaphor you can use to explain what it's like to have ADHD. It's like having erectile dysfunction of the mind. If the task you are faced with is something that turns you on, something that is interesting for you, you're 'up for it' and you can perform. But if the task is not intrinsically interesting to you, if it doesn't turn you on, you can't get up for it and you can't perform. It doesn't matter how much you tell yourself, 'I need to, I ought to.' It's just not a willpower kind of thing."

Recent research offers considerable evidence that ADHD is not a "willpower thing," even though, in many ways, it appears to be a lack of willpower. When individuals with ADHD are faced with a task that is interesting to them, not because someone told them that it ought to be interesting but because it is attractive to them at that moment, that perception, conscious or unconscious, changes the chemistry of the brain instantly, this process is not under voluntary control.

The willpower assumption is based on two fundamental misunderstandings of how the human brain works. This assumption ignores the complex and influential role of unconscious emotions in the brain's motivation processes. It does not recognize the critical importance of working memory for prioritizing tasks moment by moment.

The primary difference between Google searches and any given individual's motivations, beyond the apparent differences in the size of the information database, is the process by which relevance and prioritizing of information is determined. Google prioritizes based on the relevance of manifest content and the frequency of demand in similar searches. The primary basis on which humans prioritize information is the emotion associated with conscious and unconscious memories activated by the individual's thoughts and perceptions at any given moment.

Your Emotional Brain

In 1996, neuroscientist Joseph LeDoux, PhD, published The Emotional Brain (Commissions Earned), a book highlighting the central importance of emotion in the brain's cognitive functioning. He emphasized that mostly unconscious emotions are powerful and critically important motivators of human thought and actions. This understanding of the essential role of emotion in all aspects of human motivation and behaviour has not been adequately integrated into current thinking about ADHD.

Emotions, positive and negative, play a critical role in executive functions:

- Initiating and prioritizing tasks
- Sustaining or shifting interest or effort
- Holding thoughts inactive memory
- Choosing to avoid a job or situation

Many people think of emotions as involving only conscious feelings, limited to sensations of sadness, anger, pleasure, worry, and so on, that a person is fully aware of and generally able to identify. Neuroscience has shown that conscious feelings are only a tiny part of the variegated range of emotions that operates within each person to motivate executive functions. Neuroscientist Joaquin Fuster, M.D., emphasized, "Whereas we may be fully conscious of a retrieved memory, the vast majority of memories that we retrieve remain unconscious."

Often, these unconscious emotions conflict and cause us to act in ways inconsistent with our recognized conscious intentions. An undercurrent of conflicting emotions is often involved in our failure to do tasks that we believe we want to do, or indirectly or indirectly engaging in actions that consciously we think we do not want to do.

Sometimes a person thinks of a particular task as necessary, honestly believing that he wants to give it immediate attention and sustained effort, yet he does not act accordingly. He may continue to procrastinate, busying himself with work on other tasks that are not as urgent, or he may actively seek out distractions by getting in touch with friends, surfing the Internet, getting high, or going to sleep. Such contradictions make sense only when we realize that the emotions that guide our motivations often are not fully conscious or conflicting. We may be influenced by emotions that we do not know we have (see "Running Away from Stressful Situations," below).

Motivation Factors

The essential factor contributing to the ability of persons with ADHD to focus very well and efficiently utilize their executive functions on some tasks while being chronically unable to focus adequately on most other jobs is the neural transmission. For many years, it has been recognized that individuals with ADHD tend to chronically have insufficient release and reloading of the neurotransmitter dopamine at synaptic junctions of neurons in the networks that manage executive functions.

Many studies have demonstrated that treatment with stimulant medications improves the efficiency of neural communication. However, this increased release and slowed reloading is not under voluntary control. It occurs only for those tasks in which the individual with ADHD has a strong interest. The heightened interest maybe because that activity has brought pleasure or other rewards to the person in the past. Or who may intensify interest because the person fears that something they anticipate as unpleasant is likely to occur quickly if they do not attend to the task immediately? Whether because of anticipated pleasure or fear, the heightened interest generates an increased release of dopamine instantly and sustains it for as long as the intensified interest persists.

The second factor influencing the ability to pay attention to some tasks but not to others is the relative weakness in working memory that is characteristic of many persons with ADHD.

Working memory is essential for keeping in mind the relative priorities of our various interests at any given time.

Social psychological research has shown that individuals with larger working memory capacity are generally better able to deal with emotions, pleasant and unpleasant, without getting excessively caught up in them. Those with ADHD tend to have less "bandwidth" in their working memory functions and are likely to have more difficulty than others quickly linking together various memories relevant to doing or not doing a task.

They are less likely to consider the bigger picture of which the present moment is a part (see "Stuck in Emotion," below). They operate more like someone watching a basketball game through a telescope, unable to take into account the rest of the action on the court, the threats and opportunities that are not included in the small circle of focus provided by their telescope.

Running Away from Stressful Situations

It was a difficult exam, and Jim was having trouble answering most of the questions, possibly because he had not yet read even half of the chapters assigned for the test. Jim had put off doing any work on the exam for several days. He had been preoccupied with an email from his girlfriend back home. She wrote that she wanted to break up because he was now too far away, and she had gotten involved with someone else.

At 2 a.m., after struggling with the exam for several hours, Jim decided to take a nap for a couple of hours and try to finish the exam when he woke up. He set his alarm for 4 a.m. When the alarm buzzed, Jim woke up for a few moments, turned the alarm off, and went back to sleep. He did not wake up until five hours later.

When he realized he had slept through the deadline, Jim panicked. The professor had announced that he would not accept any late exams. Recognizing that he would undoubtedly get an F on the midterm, Jim impulsively decided he was not ready to be in college. Without discussing his decision with anyone, he packed his suitcase and left to go home, planning to stay there until the following fall, when he would try again to go to college.

In talking with me back home about this, a week later, Jim said that dropping out of college was the best thing for him at that point. He said he had been excited to go off to college, but the work seemed too hard for him, he had not yet made any real friends, and he had been missing his girlfriend and his parents. He also claimed that getting an F on the midterm would have meant failing that course, so it made no sense for him to continue using his methods that semester. He could see no other way to deal with that situation. He also mentioned that, in coming home, he had hoped he could win back his girlfriend's affections. As it turned out, she was not interested in getting re-involved with him.

It was a pattern that Jim hadn't recognized. Jim had quite many activities before. He was quick to feel unsure of himself and quick to get himself out of any situation where he was afraid he might not do well. He was biased toward early escape from stress.

Only after several months of psychotherapy was Jim able to see that his "accidental" going back to sleep that morning, his failure even to discuss his situation with his college advisor, and his assumption that he faced inevitable failure were not the best choices for him.

Stuck In Emotion

A woman told me that she dreaded Wednesday evenings. For her family, that was the night after their Wednesday morning trash pickup. She had two teenage sons, and her husband asked their boys to take on the job of dragging the trash cans down to the foot of their driveway every Tuesday evening and then to bring the emptied cans back up the driveway each Wednesday afternoon. Many times they forgot to bring the trash cans back in.

The mother explained that any time her husband got home from work on Wednesday evening and saw the trash cans still at the base of the driveway, he would become enraged and scream at them, saying they were losers, irresponsible, ungrateful for what they had been given, unwilling to help the family by doing the simple chore of bringing the trash cans back up to the house once a week.

The mother explained that each time her husband scolded their sons so harshly, he would later calm down and mumble an apology to the boys. She said, "I know he loves them both and would give his life for either one of them, but when he gets wound up in one of those Wednesday-night episodes, he gets so enraged that he seems to forget that those are his sons whom he loves and wants to protect. All he knows at that moment is that he is furious with both of them for not having done that chore."

Any parent can lose their temper with a child occasionally, but most parents, most of the time, can express their frustration to the child without such an intense verbal attack. Their working memory allows them to hold in mind their love, even while their anger takes up a lot of space in their head.

ADHD And Motivation Problems

Unfortunately, adults and children with ADHD are often labelled as unmotivated, lazy, or even apathetic. These negative labels are unfair and hurtful. Instead of simple laziness or a lack of motivation, this "immobility" or "sluggishness" often reflects the impairments in executive function associated with ADHD. Understanding these impairments is essential to correct misperceptions about ADHD that tend to run rampant.

ADHD And Executive Function

Executive function deficits affect a person's ability to get started, organize, and sustain effort on tasks. The individual may even experience a sense of paralysis associated with a task or project wanting to get started but unable to make progress forward in any manner. This sense of paralysis can quickly lead to feelings of being overwhelmed, procrastination, and avoidance, ultimately resulting in productivity problems.

It can also result in adverse reactions from others who become confused and frustrated by the inconsistencies in the person with ADHD who can perform well when the task is stimulating and exciting or novel and exciting but does not perform well when the job is tedious or repetitive.

Even if the person can begin the task, they may have great difficulty staying alert and persisting in this effort. Though they may know what they need to do to get things completed, as hard as they try, they just can't.

Boredom results in all sorts of problems for kids and adults with ADHD. Maintaining focus on a tedious task may seem nearly impossible as individuals' attention wanders away to more exciting activities and thoughts. What can also happen is that after repeated frustrations, the child or adult with ADHD can begin to feel less motivated. It can be hard to get excited and hopeful about something and then crash down again and again.

Treatments

First of all, it is essential to engage in treatment for ADHD actively. Connect with a doctor experienced in treating ADHD, and openly and regularly communicate with them about your (or your child's) symptoms.

- ADHD Coping Strategies
- Break down projects into smaller, more manageable chunks
- Set smaller goals
- Reward yourself (or your child) more immediately for little steps taken towards reaching goals
- Set aside a short, less overwhelming period (for example, 10 or 15 minutes) to commit to working on the activity that has you feeling stuck
- Exercising

Incorporate Physical Movement Into Your Day

What are some of the strategies and tips you found to help get started and sustaining focus on a task that is overwhelming or just plain boring? It always helps to hear from others on how they deal with similar issues. Then you can try more strategies and pick out the ones that work best for you.

Ways For Adults With ADHD To Get Motivated

9 Tips To Get Motivated

Living with ADHD doesn't mean completing projects or meeting deadlines. You can find ways to improve motivation without having to make sweeping lifestyle changes.

1. Set Smaller Goals: A significant goal can be daunting for anyone and can make it easier to quit before you've even begun. You may find increased motivation when you take large tasks and break them down into smaller, more achievable goals. This can also help prevent a lack of motivation over tasks that feel too long or boring.

2. Create A Task List: Lists can be great ways to get organized and define a starting point. They can also provide a visual checklist that can help progress feel more substantial.

3. Involve Others: Having someone else help hold you accountable for tasks can help get a job done. Not only can another person make the workload more accessible, but they can also help the time feel as if it passes more quickly. They are having someone to be social with may also improve your desire to complete tasks.

4. Create Rewards: Don't forget to treat yourself for a job well done, so you're more likely to complete the task in the future. If you've set small goals, try doing something you enjoy after you've successfully checked off each plan. Maybe you enjoy spending time outdoors, talking with a friend, dancing or listening to a favourite song, or having a snack. No matter how small, consider rewarding your successes each day.

5. Take The Pressure Off: Thinking that you "have to" do something might make you less likely to do it at all. Instead of telling yourself you have to do the dishes because it's expected of you, remind yourself you enjoy the look of a clean kitchen or having clean dishes readily available.

6. Change The Routine: Repetitive, familiar tasks might not quickly motivate you. In this case, try doing those tasks in a new way. If you always fold the laundry while you sit on the couch, try moving to the bedroom or standing at the dining room table for a change.

7. Visualize The Result: Projects can be less intimidating if you have a clear goal in mind. This may also help you break down a more extensive project into smaller tasks.

8. Identify Your Productive Time: Maybe you're a morning person, or maybe you feel your best right after dinner. Knowing when you're most likely to complete a task can help set you up for success.

9. Start Your Day With Success: Feelings of accomplishment are directly linked to the brain's dopamine reward system. By starting your day off with a successful simple task, you may be more likely to continue down the road of motivation.

Social Skills In Adults With ADHD

Individuals with ADHD often experience social difficulties, social rejection, and interpersonal relationship problems due to their inattention, impulsivity, and hyperactivity. Such adverse interpersonal outcomes cause emotional pain and suffering.

They also appear to contribute to the development of comorbid mood and anxiety disorders. Because very little research has been published regarding social skills in adults with ADHD, the suggestions given in this sheet are based primarily upon sound clinical practices and upward extrapolations from the research on children's social skills and ADHD.

Overall Impact Of ADHD On Social Interactions

It is not difficult to understand the reasons why individuals with ADHD often struggle in social situations. Interacting successfully with peers and significant adults is one of the most important aspects of a child's development, yet 50 to 60 per cent of children with ADHD have difficulty with peer relationships.

To interact effectively with others, an individual must be attentive, responsible, and control impulsive behaviours. Adults with ADHD are often inattentive and forgetful and typically lack impulse control. Because ADHD is an "invisible disability," often unrecognized by those unfamiliar with the disorder, socially inappropriate behaviours resulting from ADHD symptoms are often attributed to other causes.

People often perceive these behaviours and the individual who commits them as rude, self-centred, irresponsible, lazy, impolite, and a host of other negative personality attributes. Over time, such negative labels lead to social rejection of the individual with ADHD. Social rejection causes emotional pain in many children and adults who have ADHD and can create havoc and lower self-esteem throughout the life span. In relationships and marriages, inappropriate social behaviour may anger the partner or spouse without ADHD, who may eventually "burn out" and give up on the relationship or marriage.

Educating individuals with ADHD, their significant others, and their friends about ADHD and how it affects social skills and interpersonal behaviours can help alleviate much of the conflict and blame. At the same time, the individual with ADHD needs to learn strategies to become as proficient as possible in social skills. With proper assessment, treatment, and education, individuals with ADHD can learn to interact with others effectively in a way that enhances their social life.

ADHD And The Acquisition Of Social Skills

Social skills are generally acquired through incidental learning: watching people, copying the behaviour of others, practising, and getting feedback. Most people start this process during early childhood. Social skills are practised and honed by "playing grown-up" and through other childhood activities. The finer points of social interactions are sharpened by observation and peer feedback.

Children with ADHD often miss these details. They may pick up bits and pieces of appropriate but lack an overall view of social expectations. Unfortunately, as adults, they often realize "something" is missing but are never quite sure what that "something" maybe.

Social acceptance can be viewed as a spiral going up or down. Individuals who exhibit appropriate social skills are rewarded with more acceptance from those with whom they interact and are encouraged to develop even better social skills. For those with ADHD, the spiral often goes downward. Their lack of social skills leads to peer rejection, which then limits opportunities to learn social skills, which leads to more rejection, and so on. Social punishment includes denial, avoidance, and other, less subtle means of exhibiting one's disapproval towards another person.

It is important to note that people do not often let the offending individual know the nature of the social violation. Pointing out that a social skill error is being committed is often considered socially inappropriate. Thus, people are often left on their own to try to improve their social skills without understanding exactly what areas need improvement.

Specific ADHD Symptoms And Social Skills

Inattention

Tips For Identifying Subtext:

- Look for clues in your environment to help you decipher the subtext. Be mindful of alternative possibilities. Be observant.
- Be aware of body language, tone of voice, behaviour, or the look of someone's eyes to interpret better what they are saying.
- Look at a person's choice of words to better detect the subtext. ("I'd love to go" probably means yes. "If you want to" means perhaps not, but I'll do it.)
- Actions speak louder than words. If someone's words say one thing, but their actions reveal another, it would be wise to consider that their efforts might be showing their true feelings.
- Find a guide to help you with this secret language. Compare your understanding of reality with their knowledge of reality. If there is a discrepancy, you might want to try the other person's interpretation and see what happens, especially if you usually get it wrong.
- Learn to interpret polite behaviour. Polite behaviour often disguises actual feelings.

- Be alert to what others are doing. Look around for clues about proper behaviour, dress, seating, parking, and the like.

A momentary lapse in attention may result in the adult with ADHD missing critical information in social interaction. If a simple sentence like "Let's meet at the park at noon," becomes simply "Let's meet at noon," the listener with ADHD misses the crucial information about the location of the meeting. The speaker may become frustrated or annoyed when the listener asks where the meeting will occur, believing that the listener intentionally wasn't paying attention and didn't value what they had to say. Or even worse, the individual with ADHD goes to the wrong place, yielding confusion and even anger in the partner. Unfortunately, neither the speaker nor listener realizes that important information has been missed until it is too late.

A related social skills difficulty for many with ADHD involves missing the subtle nuances of communication. Those with ADHD will often have a problem "reading between the lines" or understanding subtext. It is difficult enough for most to attend to the text of conversations without the additional strain of needing to be aware of the subtext and what the person means. Unfortunately, what is said is often not what is intended.

Impulsivity

Impulsivity negatively affects social relationships because others may attribute impulsive words or actions to a lack of caring or regard for others.

Failure to stop and think first often has devastating social consequences. Impulsivity in speech, without self-editing what is about to be said, may appear as unfiltered thoughts. Opinions and views are shared in their raw form, without the usual veneer that most people use to be socially appropriate. Interruptions are common.

Impulsive actions can also create difficulties as individuals with ADHD may act before thinking through their behaviour. Making decisions based on an "at the moment" mentality often leads to poor decision-making. Those with ADHD often find themselves lured off task by something more inviting. Impulsive actions can include taking reckless chances, failure to study or prepare for school- or work-related projects, affairs, quitting jobs, making decisions to relocate, financial overspending, and even aggressive actions, such as hitting others or throwing items.

Rapid and excessive speech can also be a sign of impulsivity. The rapid-fire speech of an individual with ADHD leaves little room for others who might want to participate in the conversation. Monologues rather than dialogues go many with ADHD without satisfying relationships or needed information.

Hyperactivity

Physical hyperactivity often limits the ability to engage in leisure activities. Failure to sit still and concentrate for concerts, religious ceremonies, educational events, or even leisure vacations and the like may be interpreted by others as a lack of caring or concern for the person with ADHD. In addition, difficulties looking attentive leave others feeling unattended.

Assessment Of Social Skills

Interviews and self-report questionnaires are the primary tools for assessing social skill deficits and interpersonal interaction problems in adults with ADHD. During a diagnostic evaluation for ADHD (see What We Know, "Diagnosis of ADHD in Adults"), a mental health professional will thoroughly assess the social interactions of the adult. When questionnaires are used, it is essential to include both a self-report by the individual with ADHD and reports by spouses, significant others, and friends on a comparable version of the questionnaire. The questionnaire may include the following types of items:

- Difficulty paying attention when spoken to, missing pieces of information
- He appears to ignore others
- Difficulty taking turns in conversation (tendency to interrupt frequently)
- Difficulty following through on tasks and responsibilities

- Failure to use proper manners
- Missed social cues
- Disorganized lifestyle
- Sharing inappropriate information
- Being distracted by sounds or noises
- Become flooded or overwhelmed, shutting down
- Disorganized or scattered thoughts
- Rambling or straying off topic during conversations
- Ending a conversation abruptly

Treatment Strategies

When the social skill areas that need strengthening have been identified, obtaining a referral to a therapist or coach who understands how ADHD affects social skills is recommended (see Coaching). Medications are often helpful in managing ADHD symptoms; in many cases, an effective dose of drugs will give the adult with ADHD the boost in self-control and concentration necessary to utilize newly acquired social skills at the appropriate time. However, medications alone are usually insufficient to help gain the required skills (see Medication Management).

As discussed earlier, social skills training for children and adolescents with ADHD usually involves instruction, modelling, role-playing, and feedback in a safe setting such as a social skills group run by a therapist. In addition, arranging the environment to provide reminders has proven essential to using the correct social behaviour at the opportune moment. These findings suggest that adults with ADHD wishing to work on their social skills should consider the following elements when seeking an effective intervention. It is important to note that these treatment strategies are suggestions based on clinical practice rather than empirical research.

9 Ways To Master Social Skills

1. Knowledge: Often social skills can be significantly improved when there is an understanding of social skills and the areas in need of improvement. Reading books such as What Does Everybody Know That I Don't, ADD and Romance, or You, Your Relationship & Your ADD can provide some of that knowledge.

2. Attitude: Individuals with ADHD should have a positive attitude and be open to the growth of their social skills. It is also essential to be honest, and appreciative of feedback provided by others.

3. Goals: Adults with ADHD may want to pick and work on one goal at a time, based on a self-assessment and the assessments of others. Tackling the skill areas one at a time allows the individual to master each skill before moving on to the next.

4. The Echo: Those who struggle with missing information due to attentional difficulties during conversation may benefit from developing a system of checking with others what they heard. "I heard you say that. Did I get it right Is there more" Or an individual with ADHD could ask others to check with them after providing necessary information. “Please tell me what you heard me say.” In this way, who can avoid social errors due to inattention?

5. Observe Others: Adults with ADHD can learn a great deal by watching others do what they need to know. They may want to try selecting models both at work and their personal lives to help them grow in this area. Television may also provide role models.

6. Role-Play: Practising the skills they need with others is a good way for individuals with ADHD to receive feedback and improve their social skills.

7. Visualization: Can use visualization to gain additional practice and improve one’s ability to apply the skill in other settings. Those who need training in social skills can decide what they want to do and rehearse it in their minds, imagining using the talent in the environment they will be in with the people they will be interacting with. They can repeat this as many times as possible to help “overlearn” the skill. In this manner, they can gain experience in the “real” world, significantly increasing their success.

8. Prompts: Adults with ADHD can use prompts to stay focused on particular social skill goals. The prompts can be visual (an index card), verbal (someone telling them to be quiet), physical (a vibrating watch set every 4 minutes reminding them to be dead), or a gesture (someone rubbing their head) to help remind them to work on their social skills.

9. Increase "likeability": According to social exchange theory, people maintain relationships based on how well those relationships meet their needs. People are not precisely "social accountants," but people weigh the costs and benefits of being in relationships on some level. Many with ADHD are considered to be "high maintenance." Therefore, it is helpful to see what they can bring to relationships to help balance the equation.

Investigators have found that the following are characteristics of highly likeable people: sincere, honest, understanding, loyal, truthful, trustworthy, intelligent, dependable, thoughtful, considerate, reliable, warm, kind, friendly, happy, unselfish, humorous, responsible, cheerful, and trustful. Developing or improving any of the likeability characteristics should help one's social standing.

Although ADHD certainly brings unique challenges to social relationships, information and resources can help adults with ADHD improve their social skills. Most of this information is based on sound clinical practice and research on social skills and ADHD in children and adolescents; there is a great need to research social skills and ADHD in adults. Seek help through reading, counselling, or Coaching and, above all, build and maintain social connections.

Social Skills Training For Adult ADHD

Most people desire and enjoy social relationships. Moreover, meaningful social relationships offer many positive health benefits. However, symptoms of various psychiatric conditions interfere with forming and sustaining rewarding social relationships quickly. There are many causes for social skills deficiencies. Concerning ADHD, some social skill problems are due to a lack of attention to social cues and awareness of surroundings (often called social context). Other social difficulties are caused by ADHD habits or patterns that other people find annoying (e.g., being constantly late, interrupting, etc.).

Another tiresome interpersonal pattern is ongoing self-criticism. Many adults with ADHD feel bad about themselves because of their ADHD. They criticize themselves when they make mistakes. They often do this as a means to seek reassurance from others. Some other annoying habits repeatedly demonstrated by ADHD individuals are disorganization, repeated failures to correctly interpret others' body language or cues, and talking without listening to other people. Over time, a pattern like this can be exhausting for friends and family. Some may decide to distance themselves from the relationship.

Social skills training is a well-researched and effective therapeutic intervention. It is usually taught in small groups by clinicians who specialize in social skills training. Groups provide a natural social climate for exploration and practice. However, some books and websites offer social skills training for those who enjoy working on challenges on their own. Unlike skills training groups, the effectiveness of these independent social skill studies has not yet been determined.

Adult ADHD: The Importance Of Learning Social Skills

Previous log entries have discussed Adult Attention Deficit Disorder and its treatment. One of the significant areas of concern with Adult ADHD is the spouse's fate who does not have the disorder. Several spouses married to partners with ADHD have pleadingly expressed their frustration to me with the following exclamation: "He (She) is driving me crazy." It is for this reason that many ADHD marriages do not fare very well.

The ability to interact well with other people, including spouses, friends, and people in the workplace and the classroom, depends on the ability to:

- Be attentive
- Behave in responsible ways
- Control impulsive behaviours
- Remember essential details

All four are these abilities precisely what is lacking in those with ADHD, and that is why people feel "driven crazy" by them. On the surface, nothing seems wrong with ADHD people. For this reason, people have difficulty understanding why they act the way they do and often misinterpret their behaviours.

They are often blamed for being rude, inconsiderate, self-centred, irresponsible, lazy, and ill-mannered. People mistakenly think that these behaviours are deliberate and willful. Even those husbands and wives married to ADHD partners and knowing about the disorder tend to be in denial and insist that they are deliberately thoughtless and provocative.

More than a few people have written to us in various states of exhaustion and anger in dealing with their spouse and at the "end of their rope" about what to do.

Let's talk about some of what can be done, hoping that some marriages can find their way towards a more normalized life.

First, while the medication is an essential help in reducing many ADHD symptoms, it is not a cure for this disorder. The fact is that even after a regimen of medicine has been started, it will be necessary for the patient and their spouse to learn how to cope with this disorder. In other words, both husband and wife should know the essential skills and techniques to reduce their sources of conflict and enable the ADHD person to live a better-adjusted life. To this end, Social Skills Training is necessary. Social Skills training can be provided by either a coach or therapist specializing in this area of work.

Here Are Several Strategies That ADHD People Can Use And That Their Families Can Practice With Them:

1. Read everything you can about ADHD and developing social skills. Reading should be done by the individual with the disorder and their spouse. Remember the old saying: Knowledge is power.

2. Have a positive attitude about ADHD. The tendency is for those with the disorder to be very bright and creative. They often have a good sense of humour even though they can get depressed due to the frustrations of dealing with ADHD and its problems.

3. People with ADHD often blank out at times, missing essential pieces of information. This is why they are often late to places or fail to get to them at all. They need to ask others about what was just said, repeat the information, have a calendar or palm pilot to transcribe dates and times of events and even names of people. Upon meeting new people, it is a good idea to repeat their words.

4. It is important to observe others and the way they interact. This is called Observational Learning and is an integral part of the way we become socialized. It never stops, and we learn gestures and expressions from watching other people. ADHD people should make a conscious effort to do this and, with the help of their partner to understand what their errors are and learn new and better ways of interacting.

5. Help your partner identify those social behaviours that they are good at and develop those further. There is nothing wrong with enhancing strengths while learning new behaviours.

6. Rehearsing and role-playing social situations is another helpful way to improve social skills, and married couples can have fun with this.

Keep a sense of humour about things. A lot of what seems to go wrong when you have ADHD can be amusing. Laughter is the best medicine if you learn to laugh together. And remember, your spouse is not doing these things on purpose.

Ways ADHD Can Affect Social Skills

ADHD can make it hard for people to focus and pay attention. But it affects more than just school or work. ADHD can affect social skills, too. Here are five common social challenges people with ADHD may face and ways you can help.

1. Trouble Picking Up On Social Cues

The ADHD Link: People with ADHD might not notice how their behaviour affects other people. They may interrupt a lot and even bug people by breaking social rules.

How You Can Help: Role-play different social situations together. First, you play the other person in each scenario. Then switch roles. Finish by talking about what went well and what could be done differently.

2. Trouble Keeping Friends

The ADHD Link: People with ADHD can be intense and demanding without knowing it. They can have trouble taking turns and sharing, and friendships may burn out.

How You Can Help: Sign up for a sport or another group activity. It may be more accessible for people with ADHD to learn about "give and take" in a group setting rather than one-on-one.

3. Going Off-Topic

The ADHD Link: People with ADHD sometimes lose track of a conversation or get distracted by unrelated thoughts. They may also misinterpret what others are saying.

How You Can Help:

- Record a conversation.
- Listen to it together and talk about where you both hear someone going off-topic.
- Talk about how the conversation could have gone better.

4. Being Unreliable

The ADHD Link: People with ADHD can have trouble with planning and follow-through. That can lead other people to think they can't be counted on when doing group projects.

How You Can Help: Encourage people with ADHD to talk with the group members about how they'll divide up the work. Then help make a checklist or chart to keep track of personal progress.

5. Overreacting

The ADHD Link: ADHD can make it hard to manage emotions. People with ADHD may lash out when they're upset. Or they may have meltdowns at an age when it's no longer appropriate.

How You Can Help: Try to pay attention to feelings like anger and irritation. What does it feel like? Being mindful makes it easier to recognize when "emotional temperatures" are rising.

ADHD And SAD Treatment And Symptoms

As many as 80% of people with attention-deficit hyperactivity disorder (ADHD) will have at least one other psychiatric condition in their lifetime.1 Just as untreated ADHD can lead to unnecessary problems in everyday life; comorbid conditions can cause a tremendous amount of harm in those with ADHD if left undiagnosed and untreated.

Though any anxiety disorder can coexist with ADHD, social anxiety disorder (SAD) is one of the most common. Learning the differences between the two conditions is essential in the management and treatment.

SAD And ADHD

Anxiety disorders may occur much more frequently in people with ADHD than they do in the general population. According to the National Comorbidity Survey Replication, 47% of adults with ADHD have an anxiety disorder approximately 30% have SAD, specifically. Although experts don't know for sure why ADHD and SAD tend to occur together, some think that the factors that play a role in ADHD, genetics, environmental toxins, or premature birth, may also influence anxiety disorders.

Still, others believe that ADHD symptoms, themselves, contribute to anxiety. Often, ADHD symptoms such as inattention, hyperactivity, and impulsivity put a person at greater risk for being teased, bullied, or otherwise socially rejected. Fearing further rejection, many withdraw into themselves, avoiding any social setting that they find threatening.

ADHD vs Anxiety

If you have ADHD, it may be challenging to recognize the symptoms of anxiety. ADHD is an ongoing condition that often starts in childhood and can continue into adulthood. It can affect your ability to concentrate and may result in behavioural problems, such as:

- Hyperactivity
- Lack of attention
- Lack of impulse control
- Fidgeting and trouble sitting still
- Difficulty organizing and completing tasks

An anxiety disorder is more than just feeling occasionally anxious. It's a mental illness that is serious and long-lasting. It can make you feel distressed, uneasy, and terrified in benign or regular situations.

If you have an anxiety disorder, your symptoms may be so severe that they affect your ability to work, study, enjoy relationships or otherwise go about your daily activities.

The symptoms of ADHD are slightly different from those of anxiety. ADHD symptoms primarily involve issues with focus and concentration. Anxiety symptoms, on the other hand, include problems with nervousness and fear.

Even though each condition has unique symptoms, sometimes the two conditions mirror each other. That can make it difficult to tell whether you have ADHD, anxiety, or both.

How Can You Tell The Difference?

Though a professional evaluation is necessary, family members may tell the difference between ADHD and anxiety. The key is to watch how your symptoms present over time.

If you have anxiety, you may be unable to concentrate in situations that cause you to feel anxious. On the other hand, if you have ADHD, you'll find it challenging to focus most of the time in any situation. If you have both ADHD and anxiety, the symptoms of both conditions may seem more extreme. For example, stress can make it even more difficult for someone with ADHD to pay attention and follow through on tasks.

Understanding Comorbidity

It's not clear why there's a connection between ADHD and anxiety, and doctors don't fully understand what causes either condition. Genetics may be responsible for both conditions and may also cause comorbidity. Researchers have also observed several other states that are commonly seen alongside ADHD, including:

- Anxiety
- Depression
- Autism
- Sleep disorders
- Dyslexia
- Substance abuse
- Bipolar disorder

Possible causes for ADHD include genetics, environmental toxins, or premature birth. It's possible that these causes could also contribute to anxiety.

Symptoms

The following are all symptoms of SAD, though everyone might not experience all symptoms. Some people might exhibit symptoms in only one type of situation, while others might experience multiple symptoms in various social conditions. In some instances, these symptoms can overlap with or mirror those of ADHD:

- Self-conscious in front of other people
- Extreme fear that others will judge you
- Can worry for days or weeks before an event

- Avoidance of situations requiring social interaction and intensely uncomfortable if in a social situation
- Keeps conversation with others to a minimum
- Difficulty making or keeping friends
- Panic attacks, including shaking, blushing, nausea or sweating, when in a social situation
- Difficulty talking to others.

Unfortunately, some symptoms of SAD can be misinterpreted as ADHD symptoms, and it isn't until outward behaviours such as weight loss, sleeplessness, or refusal to attend social settings that the social anxiety becomes more apparent. As a result, SAD often goes undiagnosed in those who also have ADHD.

Treatment

There are no clear or published guidelines on how to treat co-occurring ADHD and SAD only after your doctor determines how your anxiety functions can they develop the best treatment plan to meet your needs.

For instance, if your anxiety and ADHD are functioning independently, your doctor may decide to treat both conditions simultaneously. Or they may choose to treat whichever condition is causing you the most problems first before moving on to the other state.

However, if your doctor believes that your anxiety is being caused or heavily influenced by your ADHD, your doctor may take a different approach to treatment.

Effective Treatment Exists!

Like other anxiety disorders, there is help if you have social phobia. Cognitive-behavioural therapy (CBT) has been found to help people understand triggers for anxiety and teaches techniques, such as thought logs, mindfulness, and relaxation exercises, to help control anxious feelings. Some people use medications to help manage stress. This can be especially effective when first beginning CBT.

Medications

If your anxiety is the result of ADHD, your doctor may decide to treat your ADHD first with medications, as this may reduce your anxiety symptoms. Common medications used to treat ADHD include:

Stimulants: Although stimulants primarily treat ADHD symptoms, as ADHD symptoms are controlled, you may also find some relief from your anxiety. In one study examining children and adolescents with ADHD and SAD comorbidity, Ritalin (methylphenidate) was associated with a significant improvement in both ADHD and SAD symptoms.5 A similar study found the same improvements in adults using extended-release Ritalin.

Non-stimulants: Selective norepinephrine reuptake inhibitors (SNRIs) like Strattera (atomoxetine) may target both ADHD and anxiety symptoms.

Managing Your Anxiety

An anxiety disorder is a mental condition that needs to be treated by a mental health professional. There are things you can do, though, to try to reduce your symptoms.

1. Learn Your Triggers: In some people, anxiety may be triggered by specific events, like speaking in public or calling someone on the phone. Once you've identified your triggers, work with your doctor to help develop ways to manage your anxiety in these situations. For example, preparing notes and practising a presentation may help you feel less anxious when speaking in front of others.

2. Get Seven To Eight Hours Of Sleep Every Night: Being tired may trigger anxiety or increase your risk of feeling anxious. Try to sleep for seven to eight hours every night. If you're having trouble falling asleep, try meditating or taking a warm bath before bed to help quiet your mind. Also plan to go to sleep and wake up at the same time every day. Setting a sleep schedule can be an effective way to train your body to sleep when it's time for bed.

3. Create A Schedule: If you have ADHD, you may find it hard to complete tasks. This can make anxiety worse in some people. To avoid this, create a schedule and stick to it. Expect each activity to take longer than you think. You don't want to set unrealistic goals for yourself, as this can increase anxiety.

4. Keep A Journal: Writing in a journal can help clear your mind. There's no wrong way to keep a journal. It's only meant for you, so you should feel comfortable writing down anything that's on your mind. Writing in a journal may also help you pinpoint things you want to discuss with your doctor or therapist.

5. Exercise Regularly: Exercise may help reduce anxiety the exercise reduced pressure in numerous different studies. More research is needed to understand how exercise affects anxiety entirely. Aim for 30 minutes of exercise a day. If you're new to training, start small and work your way up to longer, more intense workouts.

6. Be Patient: Treatment for anxiety can take time, and you may need to try several treatments before finding one that works for you. Be patient with your doctor and, most importantly, with yourself.

Talk Therapy

While medication has historically been the first line of treatment for ADHD, many people also benefit from non-medication therapies, especially true of people who are also living with an anxiety disorder.

Approaches such as cognitive-behavioural therapy (CBT) can address many of the underlying challenges of both ADHD and SAD, as well as the complicated symptoms that overlap between them. The goal of CBT is to provide techniques and practice for managing anxiety so that those with SAD.

A specific technique your therapist might recommend is exposure therapy, a type of CBT most often used when treating SAD, in which you and your therapist work together to gradually expose you to anxiety-provoking situations so you can develop healthy coping mechanisms and, over time, the situations elicit less fear. In other types of CBT, you can learn and practice social skills and relaxation techniques.

ADHD And Sleep

(ADHD) is a disorder that begins in childhood and encompasses symptoms of inattention, hyperactivity, and impulsivity. These symptoms interfere with functioning at school, at work, and in social situations. ADHD is present in approximately 5% of children, and it is more common in boys. For most people, the disorder continues into adulthood, though careful managing can significantly improve the quality of life for people with ADHD.

An estimated 25 to 50% of people with ADHD experience sleep problems, ranging from insomnia to secondary sleep conditions. Doctors are starting to realize the importance of treating sleep problems and their impact on ADHD symptoms and the quality of life for ADHD patients and their families.

What's The Connection Between ADHD And Sleep?

Beginning around puberty, people with ADHD are more likely to experience shorter sleep time, problems falling asleep and staying asleep, and a higher risk of developing a sleep disorder. Nightmares5 are also common in children with ADHD, especially those with insomnia. Sleep problems in ADHD tend to increase with age, though sleep problems in early childhood are a risk factor for the future occurrence of ADHD symptoms.

Even those who are rarely hyperactive during the day may experience racing thoughts and a burst of energy at night that interferes with sleep. For some, nighttime presents the perfect opportunity to "hyperfocus" on a project, as there are fewer distractions. Unfortunately, this makes it challenging to settle down for sleep, leading to a disrupted sleep-wake schedule. Over time, insomnia may worsen as people start to develop feelings of stress related to bedtime. Many people with ADHD experience daytime sleepiness and difficulty waking up as a result of poor sleep. Others experience restless, non-refreshing sleep with multiple nighttime awakenings.

Sleep problems in ADHD appear to differ depending on the type of ADHD. Individuals with predominantly inattentive symptoms are more likely to have a later bedtime, while those predominantly hyperactive-impulsive symptoms are more likely to suffer from insomnia. Those with combined hyperactive-impulsive and distracted ADHD experience both poor sleep quality and a later bedtime.

Many ADHD symptoms are similar to symptoms of sleep deprivation. Among others, adult ADHD sleep problems include forgetfulness and difficulty concentrating. In children, fatigue may present as being hyperactive and impulsive8. Sometimes it can be difficult to tell whether these issues are brought on by ADHD or by a lack of sleep. This may lead to misdiagnoses or may allow sleep disorders to go undetected. Experts, therefore, recommend screening patients for sleep problems before prescribing medication for ADHD.

What's The Biology Behind The ADHD-Sleep Connection?

ADHD sleep problems may be a side effect of impaired arousal, alertness, and regulation circuits in the brain. Other researchers believe that ADHD sleep problems can be traced to a delayed circadian rhythm with a later onset of melatonin production9. Despite similarities between certain sleep disorders and ADHD symptoms, research has failed to find consistent sleep abnormalities in people with ADHD.

Some individuals find it easier to sleep with the calming effects of stimulant medications commonly prescribed for ADHD. However, for many people, stimulant medications cause several sleep problems in their own right. Coexisting disorders such as anxiety, depression, or substance abuse and poor sleep hygiene will likely also play a role in sleep difficulties.

How Do ADHD Sleep Problems Affect Daily Life?

Though there is little research on ADHD with accompanying sleep disorders, children and adults with ADHD plus a sleep disorder often report more severe ADHD symptoms and a lower quality of life. They may also be more likely to suffer from depression, anxiety, hyperactivity, inattention, difficulty processing information, and a higher BMI. Over the long term, chronic sleep deprivation leaves people vulnerable to physical health problems.

Daytime sleepiness can have severe effects on school and work. People may judge a person with ADHD for sleeping at inappropriate times without realizing that it is part of their condition and challenging to avoid. Sudden bouts of sleepiness may also be dangerous while driving or performing other activities that require concentration.

Not sleeping well at night can also cause daytime fatigue. Individuals with ADHD-related sleep deprivation may feel grumpy, irritable, restless, or tired, or they may have trouble paying attention at school or work. Sometimes, these symptoms may be mistaken for a mood disorder. In turn, anxiety and behavioural difficulties have been linked to a higher incidence of sleep problems for children with ADHD.

These problems also take their toll on families and caregivers of people with ADHD. Preliminary research shows that primary caregivers of children with ADHD and sleep problems are more likely to be depressed, anxious, stressed, and late to work.

What Sleep Disorders Commonly Occur In People With ADHD?

In addition to generalized insomnia, people with ADHD have higher-than-normal rates of certain sleep disorders. Because ADHD symptoms often resemble the symptoms of these sleep disorders, underlying sleep disorders may go undiagnosed. Children, in particular, may have difficulty conveying what they are feeling, leading to a misdiagnosis of ADHD when their problems stem from a sleep disorder. Or, they may have ADHD plus a sleep disorder.

1. Circadian Rhythm Sleep Disorder: Most individuals with ADHD, particularly adolescents, are more alert in the evening. This atypical schedule can make it challenging to honour work or school commitments. A minor pineal gland, irregularities in clock genes, and later melatonin release may be responsible for circadian rhythm sleep disorders in people with ADHD. Taking melatonin supplements at targeted times or using bright light therapy may help adjust your schedule.

2. Sleep-Disordered Breathing: Sleep-disordered breathing (SDB), including snoring and sleep apnea, affects up to one-third of patients with ADHD. SDB leads to disturbed sleep and daytime sleepiness and often causes symptoms typical of ADHD. The encouraging news is that treating SDB may reduce the need for stimulants in children believed to have ADHD. Studies suggest that removing the tonsils10 may help with ADHD and sleep apnea symptoms in children, while CPAP devices are a better choice for adults.

3. Restless Legs Syndrome: People with restless legs syndrome (RLS) are plagued by tingling sensations in the legs that make it hard to fall asleep. RLS or other types of periodic limb movement disorders may occur in almost 50% of people with ADHD. Children with ADHD and RLS appear to spend longer in stage one light sleep11, which is not stimulating.

4. Narcolepsy: Individuals with narcolepsy tend to fall asleep suddenly during the day and may have difficulty sleeping soundly at night. Adults with narcolepsy are twice as likely to have had ADHD as a child. While the link between the two isn't clear, researchers believe that the sleepiness brought on by narcolepsy might provoke ADHD symptoms. It's also possible that both disorders might stem from a similar cause, such as a faulty gene or a problem with neurotransmitters. Narcolepsy is usually treated with medication.

Treating underlying sleep disorders is an essential step toward improving sleep for people with ADHD. Ask your doctor for a sleep study to rule out any secondary sleep disorders that may need to be treated along with your ADHD. A good doctor should monitor potential sleep problems regularly, as these tend to develop over time.

Sleep Tips For Children And Adults With ADHD And Sleep Problems

Experts are cautiously optimistic that sleep intervention may be vital to improving sleep and ADHD symptoms and the effects of ADHD medication. Indeed, preliminary studies have found that behavioural sleep interventions improve sleep, ADHD symptoms, quality of life, daily functioning, behaviour, and working memory.

For children, adolescents, and adults with ADHD, a consistent bedtime routine and healthy sleep hygiene practices can help reinforce the connection between bed and sleep. Try making gradual changes and note where you see improvements to develop a system that works for you. Some tips include:

- Cut out sugar, caffeine, and alcohol within a few hours of bedtime
- Avoid screen time for an hour before bed
- Avoid doing stimulating activities and projects that require hyper-focusing in the evening.
- Make the bed a stress-free zone reserved for sleep and sex
- Get enough exercise and sunlight during the day
- Develop a bedtime routine that you enjoy, such as rereading a favourite book, spending time with pets, or taking a warm bath
- Keep the bedroom dark, calm, and quiet, using a white noise machine if necessary to block out intrusive noises.
- Go to bed and wake up at the same time every day, choosing a time that is realistic and age-appropriate to get the recommended sleep for your age group.
- Use a weighted ball blanket.

People with ADHD also frequently have trouble waking up in the morning. For help getting out of bed, try using light therapy or plan something enjoyable for when you get out of bed, such as exercise or an excellent breakfast.

The Children and Adults with ADHD organization recommend using a rewards-based system for sleep problems in young children with ADHD. It may also help to offer reassurance by frequently checking on your child. For people of any age with ADHD, talking with a trusted confidant, keeping a worry journal, or using relaxation techniques such as guided imagery may help make bedtime less stressful.

Sleep medication may not be appropriate for people with ADHD, but you can talk to your doctor about adding supplements or tweaking your medication schedule to optimize it for sleep. Some people with ADHD find it helps alertness to take their medication about an hour before waking up. Adolescents and adults with sleep problems may benefit from cognitive behavioural therapy for insomnia (CBT-I).

What You Can Do

If you have ADHD and trouble sleeping, you should tell your doctor. You might need a change in your medications to make sleeping more accessible, or you might do a sleep study to see if there is another underlying cause of your sleeplessness.

If you've ruled out other causes, then your ADHD symptoms may be to blame. You may be able to improve your rest by doing the following healthy habits and routines. You should:

- Avoid napping 4 hours before bedtime.
- Avoid drinking caffeine 4 hours before bedtime.
- If you take stimulant medication, make sure you are taking it as early as possible.
- Have a calming bedtime routine.
- Go to bed at about the same time every day.
- Sleep in a comfortable bed in a dark and quiet room.
- Avoid looking at screens (T.V.s, smartphones, etc.) And electronic media in the evening.

Treatment For Sleep Disorders

In people with ADHD, it's essential to establish a suitable treatment plan for sleep disorders. This often involves psychotherapy or medical treatments that help promote normal sleep.

Some Standard Psychotherapy Techniques Include:

- Cognitive-behavioural therapy (CBT), which can show you how to manage or eliminate feelings of anxiety and thoughts that keep you from falling asleep

- Relaxation techniques, such as meditation and deep breathing exercises, which can help reduce stress before bedtime
- Stimulus control, which can teach you how to limit the time you spend in bed while not sleeping so you only associate your bed with sleep
- Sleep restriction, where you intentionally limit the time that you spend in bed lying awake or not sleeping
- Light therapy, which can help reset your internal clock so that you fall asleep at a later or more appropriate time

Some Medical Treatments That Can Help With Sleep Disorders Include:

- Prescription sleeping pills, such as zolpidem (Ambien), eszopiclone (Lunesta), or zaleplon (Sonata)
- Calcium channel blockers and muscle relaxers, which can help those with RLS
- A continuous positive airway pressure (CPAP) machine, which helps keep airways open and prevents sleep apnea
- Oral appliances, which can help to keep the throat open and to avoid sleep apnea

Lifestyle Changes And Home Remedies

- Making certain lifestyle adjustments is also essential.
- Some lifestyle changes and home remedies that can help with sleep disorders include:

- Going to bed and waking up at the same time every day, even on weekends
- Avoiding caffeine in the late afternoon and evenings
- Avoiding alcohol and nicotine close to bedtime
- Avoiding the use of electronics before bedtime
- Using the bed primarily for sleeping and never for activities like working
- Keeping the bedroom dark, quiet, and cool
- Getting enough exercise during the day
- Avoiding heavy meals close to bedtime
- Establishing a relaxation routine before bed, such as reading, doing yoga, or taking a warm bath
- Use a weighted blanket

CHAPTER 8: EMOTIONAL DYSREGULATION

ADHD And Emotional Dysregulation

Emotional symptoms are increasingly considered a core feature of attention-deficit/hyperactivity disorder (ADHD). We aimed to quantify the evidence of emotional dysregulation and its respective facets in individuals with adult ADHD compared to healthy controls using meta-analysis. Attention Deficit Hyperactivity Disorder (ADHD) is characterized by its core symptoms inattention, impulsivity, and hyperactivity. The past decade of research revealed that ADHD persists into adulthood. Apart from the core symptoms, emotion regulation contributes independently to functional impairments in patients with ADHD.

In this regard, several studies reported that emotion dysregulation (E.D.) (subsuming symptoms like low frustration tolerance, irritability, ease of negative emotional experience, and emotional lability) is widespread in children, adolescents, and adults with ADHD (; meta-analysis by and qualitative reviews by. About 70% of adult patients with ADHD report E.D. or emotional lability. Furthermore, E.D. also exists in patients with ADHD not suffering from any other comorbid mental disorder. Those findings reveal E.D. as a core component of the condition or an essential feature in a subgroup of patients with ADHD.

Two decades after Wender recognized features of E.D. as part of the clinical presentation of adult ADHD, DSM-5 refrains from including such symptoms as indicative of the disorder. Instead, the DSM-5 recommends considering E.D. as an associated feature of ADHD supporting its diagnosis. According to Kring and Sloan, such a limitation occurred because E.D. is still a transdiagnostic concept and can be applied to psychopathological aspects of various disorders not limited to ADHD. Although focusing on emotion regulation and dysregulation might provide:

- New insights into the underlying pathophysiological mechanisms
- A more accurate differentiation of symptoms and disorders
- Novel treatment approaches.

Research on E.D. still lacks a consensual and refined definition and depiction of E.D. and related constructs in general and theoretical frameworks and conceptual models of E.D. in ADHD in particular. Terms like E.D., emotional lability, emotional instability (i.e., erratic shifting between emotional states), and emotional impulsivity (i.e., overshooting emotional responses) are often applied interchangeably or instead idiosyncratically.

This lack of consensus and clarity regarding the construct of emotion regulation and E.D. summarises and integrates empirical findings in ADHD complicated. To avoid working in "conceptual and definitional chaos", we briefly define emotion regulation, E.D., and facets of E.D. that contribute to functional and psychosocial impairments in patients with ADHD.

Emotion regulation includes all processes that unfold over time and are related to people's different emotions, the intensity of emotions, and how emotions are experienced and expressed. The primary function of E.R. is to shape emotional states to facilitate adaptive, goal-directed behaviour in a particular situation. The most prominent model of emotion regulation is the modal model that proposes five types of emotion-regulation strategies:

- Taking steps to influence which situation one will be exposed to (situation selection)
- Changing relevant aspects of the situation (situation modification)
- Influencing which portions of the situation are perceived and attended to (attentional deployment)
- Altering the way of thinking about it (reappraisal)
- Directly modifying emotion-related actions (response modulation). To apply such emotion regulation strategies, emotions need to be recognized (i.e., perception and awareness of the self and other's verbal and nonverbal feelings).

Emotional Dysregulation And ADHD

Individuals with ADHD often experience difficulties regulating their emotions. These challenges are thought to have the most significant impact on an individual with ADHD's wellbeing and self-esteem, far more than the core symptoms of ADHD (hyperactivity-impulsivity and inattention).

Emotional dysregulation can be defined as an inability to modulate one's emotional experience and expression, which results in an excessive emotional response. This exaggerated response is considered inappropriate for the individual's developmental age and the social setting in which it occurs.

ADHD related emotional dysregulation is thought to result from poor executive function control, which contributes to an individual having (Barkley, 2015):

- Highly volatile emotional trigger sensitivity and emotional impulsivity due to lacking self-restraint. Emotional impulsivity contributes to ADHD symptoms such as impatience and low frustration tolerance, quickness to anger/reactive aggression/temper outbursts, and emotional liability.
- Problems self-regulating their primary emotional response. Individuals with ADHD can experience such intense, overwhelming direct emotional reactions that they find it difficult to inhibit the expression of this

emotion or moderate the feeling and replace it with a secondary emotional response.

- Problems refocusing their attention away from strong emotions. An inability to refocus attention away from strong feelings can make it challenging to reduce or moderate a primary emotional response. Refocusing problems can also contribute to thought rumination.
- Difficulties self-soothing to moderate their primary emotional response due to poor working memory (i.e. reduced ability to use self-speech and visual imagery).
- Difficulties organizing and executing an appropriate secondary response due to problems appraising, flexibly manipulating, collecting information; generating and appraising alternative responses and their possible outcomes; and planning an appropriate response.

As A Result, Individuals With ADHD Are More Likely To:

experience and display emotions more intensely, particularly during interpersonal interactions possibly due to being overwhelmed by the emotion:

- Become overly excited
- Focus on the more negative aspects of a task or situation
- Express frustration or anger and become verbally or physically aggressive

- Experience problems in social relationships, including social rejection, bullying, and isolation
- Experience relationship and marital problems, relationship breakup and divorce
- Have difficulties achieving work or academic goals/requirements, receive a school suspension or expulsion, lose their job or fail to be promoted
- Be involved in road rage and car accidents
- Report increased psychological distress from their emotional experience
- Develop anxiety and depression
- Have conduct problems, be involved in crime, and be institutionalized.

Emotional Dysregulation And Parenting Stress

Children with ADHD have been shown to increase the amount of stress experienced by parents significantly. This is further increased when the child has emotional regulation problems. Parents who experience extreme stress levels may suffer psychologically and may therefore be less able to implement the types of interventions required to help their children (Theule et al., 2011).

Emotions And ADHD

Many people with ADHD experience emotions differently to others, with many reporting:

- Fast-building, high-intensity, and short-lived emotions
- Difficulties recognizing emotions in themselves and others
- Extremes of empathizing completely with others or reacting without feelings to others
- Experiencing many more emotions simultaneously than a typical person might

Experiencing multiple contradictory emotions at the same time can be difficult for people with and without ADHD to understand. For example, it is not uncommon for someone with ADHD to say they feel excited, happy, frustrated, and nervous all at once in a situation where someone neurotypical is likely only to be experiencing one or two emotions.

Differences in emotions in people with ADHD can lead to 'shutdowns', where someone is overwhelmed with emotions that they space out, may find it hard to speak or move, and may struggle to articulate what they feel until they can process their feelings.

Similarly, people with ADHD can also experience 'meltdowns' more commonly than others, which is where emotions build up so high that someone acts out, often crying, angering, laughing, yelling, and moving all at once, driven by many different emotions at once this essentially resembles a child tantrum and can continue throughout adulthood. Meltdowns can be an important way to self-regulate and can bring great lasting relief to adults afterwards.

Differences in emotions as well as experiencing meltdowns and shutdowns are also common in autism. These differences in emotions are often referred to as' emotional dysregulation. There is an ongoing debate in the medical field about the role of ADHD in symptoms of emotional dysregulation.

Is Emotional Dysregulation Part Of ADHD?

Emotional dysregulation used to be considered a core part of ADHD and was always included in descriptions of ADHD. There have been many name changes to ADHD, with medical literature from the 19th and 20th century referring to 'minimal brain dysfunction', 'defect in moral control', 'mental restlessness', 'hyperactive child syndrome' and 'hyperkinetic impulse disorder' before the term ADHD became centralized. In all of these early conceptualizations, emotional dysregulation was considered a crucial part of ADHD. Physicians sought to treat patients and mediate the impact emotional dysregulation had on someone's life.

In the 1970s, ADHD research became more formalized to incorporate ADHD into the DSM (Diagnostic and Statistics Manual the critical psychiatry book). Emotional dysregulation was repeatedly observed during the examination, but researchers focused on inattention, hyperactivity, and impulsivity. These traits were far easier to measure and develop treatments for in a laboratory or clinical setting. Measuring emotional dysregulation was more challenging and, as such, it was phased out of medical descriptions of ADHD.

What Is Known About Emotional Dysregulation And ADHD Now?

Despite being left out of the DSM, emotional dysregulation continued to show up in ADHD research. Researchers today are unanimous in agreement that ADHD and emotional dysregulation are strongly connected. There are debates over how emotional dysregulation relates to ADHD, however. The opposing models are:

Emotional dysregulation is a core trait of ADHD. The same brain and nervous system change to features like impulse control, executive function, and working memory like how inattention, hyperactivity, and impulsivity arise from these changes.

Emotional dysregulation is a separate condition from ADHD. It comes from the different, but overlapping brain and nervous system changes, meaning people with ADHD are much more likely to develop emotional dysregulation like how people with ADHD are also expected to grow dyslexia.

Emotional dysregulation and ADHD together comprise a new condition distinct from ADHD altogether. Some people also believe that emotional dysregulation in ADHD is strictly due to other mental health conditions that can co-occur with ADHD. Whilst co-occurring conditions can create a research challenge and weaken data, and this idea has been disproven.

Emotional Sensitivities And ADHD

Emotional self-control, particularly related to difficult emotions like frustration, anger, or sadness, can be very challenging for someone with ADHD. It is painful to experience negative feelings so profoundly and have little ability to control your response. What's more, emotional sensitivities can often affect social interactions when others are on the receiving end of these strong emotions.

When a person is impulsive, they simply react driven by the intensity of the moment. To delay a response allows a person to separate a bit from the emotions and respond more objectively. This ability to postpone response is sometimes challenging for those with ADHD.

At this point, it is unclear whether the symptoms related to emotional dysregulation are caused by ADHD itself, or comorbid psychiatric conditions, which many people with ADHD have. It is also possible that because of past experiences and growing up with all the negative labels that can associate with ADHD, some people with ADHD may simply feel more sensitive to negative statements or complaints or even gentle suggestions from others than a person who did not grow up with ADHD.

ADHD And Physical Sensitivities

Many people with ADHD are also hypersensitive to their physical surroundings. Sounds as subtle as the humming of the air conditioning or lights from a flickering candle or the scratching from a tag on a shirt can become major distractions. When a person cannot filter and inhibit their responses to incoming stimuli like sights and sounds, everything becomes a distraction.

Instead of having problems with inattention, this person may pay attention to everything, whether it is relevant or not. This can be very disorienting. Difficulties integrating sensory input may also contribute to physical sensitivities.

A simple pat on the shoulder from a caring teacher may feel irritating to some students with ADHD. As a result, the reaction creates problems for this child and confusion for the teacher. For adults with ADHD, these sensitivities around touch and sensory stimulation can also make quite a few difficulties in intimate relationships.

Coping With Hypersensitivity In ADHD

While hypersensitivity and heightened emotions can feel like a burden at times, you can learn techniques to help you cope and use these traits to your advantage. People with ADHD are often very creative and empathetic, characteristics that can be significant assets.

Awareness and understanding of these sensitivities often associated with ADHD is an excellent first step, recognizing that they are part of your disorder rather than simply being overly emotional. This can help you avoid unnecessary and unconstructive self-criticism.

CHAPTER 9: ADHD AND SEXUALITY

Attention deficit hyperactivity disorder (ADHD) is a neurological condition that causes impulsivity, hyperactivity, and a lack of focus. ADHD comes with a slew of stereotypes (e.g., little kids running up and down the aisle on a plane), but the condition looks different in adults.

Those with ADHD may struggle with:

- Time management
- Concentration
- Self-discipline
- Organization
- Misplaced motivation
- Susceptibility to addiction
- Self-regulation of emotions

Misunderstood

Healthy relationships and good sex are the result of emotionally present, confident partners. But confidence can diminish after years of dealing with the stigma and other difficulties of ADHD. Adults with ADHD may have trouble maintaining professional and personal stability and may seem forgetful, distracted, and inattentive to those around them. Romantic partners may feel responsible for all household tasks because they can't depend on the person who has ADHD. These frustrations can lead to depression, anxiety, and emotional turbulence for people living with ADHD and may manifest as one of two types of sexual behaviour: hypersexuality or hyposexuality.

Hypersexuality And ADHD

An unusually high sex drive characterizes hypersexuality. It happens because sexual stimulation boosts endorphin production and brain activity, both of which create a sense of calm. When a person dealing with ADHD finds an (ahem) activity that reduces their restlessness and helps them feel calm, they may seek it out to an extreme degree. Hanky-panky is good for the soul, but problematic pornography use and a constant need for sex can lead to relationship troubles. And because some people with ADHD have difficulty with impulse control, they're at a higher risk for substance abuse, which could further affect their decision-making.

Hyposexuality And ADHD

Hyposexuality is hypersexuality's sleepy cousin: It's the loss of desire for sex. People experiencing hyposexuality may be too distracted to carry out the "task" in front of them. While hyposexuality may be a symptom of ADHD, it can also be a side effect of antidepressants or other medications prescribed to manage ADHD. Talk to your doctor if you think medication could be affecting your sex drive. They can help you find an alternative.

Hypersensitivity And ADHD

Some people with ADHD experience high sensitivity to physical sensations, making typically très agréable pastimes uncomfortable or even painful. Touch isn't the only sense that may be an issue. Smell and taste can also be heightened, causing a person with ADHD to become distracted, overwhelmed, and unable to enjoy the moment.

Hyperactivity

Hyperactivity, a symptom closely associated with ADHD, might also affect a person's sex life. People with ADHD may find it difficult to relax or unwind, making it hard for them to become aroused. They may also feel the need to switch positions frequently or be unable to stay focused long enough to have sex.

What Effect Does ADHD Have On Sexuality?

Attention deficit hyperactivity disorder (ADHD) causes a range of symptoms, including hyperactivity, difficulty paying attention, and behavioural problems. ADHD may also affect romantic relationships, feelings of self-worth, or even the ability to perform sexually.

These markers are not used to make a diagnosis, and they may be due to the disorder itself or develop as a side effect of medicines used for treatment.

Though ADHD is frequently diagnosed in childhood, it affects the lives of many adults. Some adults with ADHD report experiencing changes in their sex life.

Crouching Tiger, Hidden Orgasms

Women and men experience ADHD differently, but women may have an extra hurdle in relaxing or focusing enough to reach orgasm. Though some women can orgasm easily and often, many need to feel relaxed to get there, making it extremely difficult for those with ADHD. However, anyone with ADHD may have issues reaching orgasm due to trouble focusing or side effects of medications.

Improving Sex With ADHD: Just The Tip(S)

"C" Is For Communication

Even when ADHD isn't a factor, sex is best when partners know how to please each other. This isn't a silent movie, people. Say what you like! Let your partner know what you need! This is especially true for those with ADHD.

Communicating any sexual issues beforehand and letting your partner know what they can do will help prevent confusion and hurt feelings. If it's a matter of hypersensitivity, again, communication is critical. Hopefully, the partner without ADHD will (hopefully) care a lot more about getting their partner to orgasm than lighting that Cinnamon Explosion scented candle on the nightstand.

Spice Up Your Life

Sometimes the best way to get out of a sex rut is to mix things up. If you find you're having trouble focusing in the bedroom, discuss some ways to make sex more exciting with your partner. Try new positions. Buy a new toy. Have spontaneous sex in the kitchen. Role-play. Incorporate new things into your sex life and see if any of them stick.

Be In The Moment

Meditation, yoga, and mindfulness can help people with ADHD focus on the present. Taking a meditation or yoga class can be helpful because the group setting is free from the plentiful distractions at home.

Mindfulness is a practice that can apply to everything from sex to cooking. It involves mentally checking in with your body and soul throughout the day, so you're aware of distractions, negative behaviours, and underlying emotions.

Be Nice To Yourself

People dealing with ADHD may have internalized the thought that their symptoms are personal flaws, leading to low self-esteem. Treat yourself with some TLC. Shame and self-loathing won't help you feel sexy. Accept your limits and know that everyone has their own. Frequently remind yourself (or your partner) that everyone deserves to be loved and sexually satisfied, even if the house is a mess or you've been reading the same page for 10 minutes because your mind keeps wandering. Lean in.

Sexy Time

Schedule sex dates with your partner. Put them in your calendar and highlight them in red. Planning for sex may not feel sexy, but if spontaneity is the issue of getting aroused and you need some time to get your head (and body) in the game, give yourself time to prepare mentally.

Avoid Sensations

Romance and sexuality can involve the use of many senses, such as smell and touch. However, these sensations may not be suitable for people with ADHD who are hypersensitive. For example, scented candles, incense, or massage oils may be too distracting for some people, while others might be sensitive to light or sounds. When a person identifies what does and does not work for them, they should let their partner know, which should help create a welcoming sexual atmosphere.

Remove Distractions

While some people find mood music or background noise calming, someone with ADHD might find it distracting. Turning off the television, radio, or computer during sex may help avoid these distractions. However, distractions can range from the sound of a fan in the room to the sight of an unfinished project on the table. These distractions may be enough to reduce arousal in some people. Again, communication is essential. When people know what distraction to avoid, they may find their romantic moments are more present and focused.

Make Changes

For people who appear to be losing interest in sex, making changes in their sexual play, techniques, or even locations may provide enough stimuli to improve arousal and increase their sexual satisfaction. Always communicate this to the sexual partner, but changing the sexual routine may be the way forward for some people.

Focus On Being Present

Practising mindfulness exercises such as meditation or yoga may help to calm a person before sex. Making an effort to stay focused on what is happening at the moment may help keep a person's mind from straying. Learning to focus takes practice, and mindfulness activities, such as meditation, breathing exercises, or yoga, maybe a good place to start. Doing these activities with a partner before sex may help calm both people down, allowing them to enter a more relaxed state.

Scheduling

Sometimes, who may overcome problems with sex by setting a schedule and sticking to it? Scheduling sex may sound unromantic, but it may put some people's minds at ease. Knowing that they have a specific time to focus on sex may help ease a person's anxiety or help them prepare for it.

How ADHD Can Affect Your Sex Life

There are many ways that attention deficit hyperactivity disorder (ADHD) can affect your sex life. If you live with ADHD, you might notice that you are hypersensitive to sensory stimulation, making sensual touch feel irritating and even annoying. Or perhaps your level of sexual desire changes drastically from one day to the next.

On the flip side, some people with ADHD have such a high sex drive and need for stimulation and novelty, such as pornography, that it causes problems in a partnership. People with ADHD may also be prone to sexual risk-taking such as unprotected sex or having multiple sex partners. The disorder is associated with a drop in neurotransmitters, leading to these types of impulsive behaviours.

What To Do If Your Partner Has ADHD

As the partner of someone living with this disorder, you might notice that your partner becomes distracted during intercourse and quickly loses focus and interest, which you might interpret as rejection. It's important to understand that ADHD causes trouble concentrating in many areas of life, and sex is often no exception. It usually has nothing to do with the person's interest in their partner.

Let's not forget, the exaggerated feelings that someone with ADHD may experience, such as anger and frustration, can create feelings of conflict in any romantic relationship. This conflict can result in difficulties connecting sexually as well.

ADHD And Marriage

ADHD can cause problems in romantic relationships and marriages if it's left untreated or not talked about.

People who have ADHD tend to have issues with:

- Financial responsibility
- Household chores
- Good judgment
- Conflict resolution
- Impulsive behaviour

Because of this, the partner of someone with ADHD may feel like the burden of household tasks falls only on their shoulders (lest we forget this iconic scene from "Mrs. Doubtfire").

They may feel more like a parent than a partner to their S.O., and nothing screams "HOT SEX" less than having to ask someone to clean up after themself 20 times or not being able to fully trust them to watch the kids when you're not there.

If left unresolved, these issues can lead to separation or divorce.

It's important to remember that if this type of behaviour stems from ADHD, it may require time, patience, empathy, and often medication and therapy to manage. What may seem like a lack of effort or love or just irresponsible behaviour is not intentional.

But all the empathy in the world can't curb feelings of chaos and unfairness when you feel like you're on your own in a partnership. Consider going to couples' counselling sooner rather than later.

Ways To Boost Intimacy In An ADHD Marriage

1. Touch each other. Every day, do something that connects you physically to your partner: Hold her hand, wash her hair, massage his sore feet, and so on. Be sure to hug each other, too.

2. Make regular dates with one another no matter how busy you are or how children seem to get in the way. Set your alarm clock 10 minutes early each morning, and use the time to cuddle and share positive emotions.

3. Send romantic notes. Place them where your partner will happen upon them-in his briefcase, for example, or on the bathroom mirror.

Couples' Therapy

We all need a fresh perspective from time to time. A couple coping with ADHD will have obstacles other couples may not, but that doesn't mean they can't improve. To revive their sex life, both parties may need to adjust the way they deal with ADHD, whether it's their own or their partner's.

Not Sure If It's Time For Therapy? It May Be Time If Your Relationship Is Faltering Due To:

- A lacklustre (or nonexistent) sex life
- A messy house that affects the mood of one or more people
- Financial issues, due in part to disorganization and poor management
- Incessant fighting

The partner who has (or may have) ADHD may want to see a specialist and begin a treatment plan if they haven't already. Couples' counselling with a therapist who specializes in ADHD will provide extra support.

Things To Remember If You Love A Person With ADD/ADHD

It's a fact; a person with ADD is hard to love. You never know what to say. It's like walking through a minefield. You tiptoe around, unsure which step (or word) will be the one that sets off an explosion of emotion. It's something you try to avoid.

People who have ADD/ADHD are suffering. Life is more difficult for them than the average person. Everything is intense and magnified. Their brilliant minds are constantly in gear, creating, designing, thinking, and never resting. Imagine what it would feel like to have a merry-go-round in your mind that never stops spinning.

From emotional outbursts to polar opposite extremes, ADD presents several behaviours that can be harmful to relationships. ADD is a mysterious condition of opposites and extremes. For instance, when it comes to concentration, people with ADD cannot concentrate when they are emotional or when their thoughts are distracted. However, when they are interested in a specific topic, they zone in so deep that it's hard to pull them out of that zone. Starting a project is a challenge, but stopping it is an even more significant challenge.

True love is unconditional, but ADD presents situations that test your limits of love. Whether it's your child, boyfriend, girlfriend, spouse, or soon-to-be spouse, ADD tests every relationship. The best way to bring peace into both your lives is to learn a new mindset to deal with the emotional roller-coaster that ADD brings all-day-every-day.

Understanding what a person with ADD feels like will help you become more patient, tolerant, compassionate, and loving. Your relationships will become more enjoyable and peaceful. This is what goes on in the mind of a person with ADD/ADHD:

1. They Have An Active Min: The ADD brain doesn't stop. There's no on/off switch. There are no brakes that bring it to a halt. It is a burden that one must learn to manage.

2. They Listen But Don't Absorb What Is Being Said: A person with ADD will look at you, hear your words, watch your lips move, but after the first five words, their mind is on a journey. They can still listen to you speak, but their thoughts are in outer space. They are thinking about how your lips are moving or how your hair is out of place.

3. They Have Difficulty Staying On Task: Instead of focusing on what's in front of them, people with ADD stare at the colours in the painting on the wall. Like walking through a labyrinth, they start moving in one direction but keep changing demands to find the way out.

4. They Become Anxious quickly: As deep thinkers, they are sensitive to whatever is going on around them. Being in a noisy restaurant can sound like you are standing in the front row at a Metallica concert. A depressing news snippet can set them into end-of-the-world mode.

5. They Can't Concentrate When They Are Emotional: If there is something problematic or upset, someone with ADD cannot think of anything else. This makes concentration on work, conversation, and social situations almost impossible.

6. They Concentrate Too Intensely: When the doors of their mind open, the person with ADD dives in like a scuba diver jumping into the deep ocean.

7. They Have Difficulty Stopping A Task When They Are In The Zone: And under the deep ocean, they stay for hours. Even when their oxygen is running low, they won't come up for air until they're almost out of oxygen if they are enjoying the view.

8. They Cannot Regulate Their Emotions: For a person with ADD, their emotions fly wild, out of proportion, and cannot be contained. The tangled wires in their brilliant brains make thought and feelings difficult to process. They need extra time to get their systems up and running correctly.

9. They Have Verbal Outbursts: Their intense emotions are hard to regulate. Since they impulsively say whatever they think, they often say things they later regret. It's almost impossible for them to edit their words before they release them.

10. They Have Social Anxiety: Feeling uncomfortable knowing that they are different, people with ADD are often uncomfortable in social situations. They are afraid they will say something foolish or react inappropriately. Holding back feels safer.

11. They Are Deeply Intuitive: For people with ADD, the surface is an invisible exterior that they penetrate. They see beyond it. This is the most enjoyable aspect of ADD. This inspirational trait is what makes creative geniuses. Inventors, artists, musicians, and writers thrive in this zone.

12. They Think Out Of The Box: Another remarkable aspect of ADD is that because they think differently, their abstract minds see solutions to problems that the concrete thinker cannot see.

13. They Are Impatient And Fidgety: Annoyed quickly, wanting things to happen immediately, and constantly playing with their phones, twirling their hair, or bouncing their leg up and down; a person with ADD needs constant motion. It's a calming Zen activity for them.

14. They Are Physically Sensitive: Pencils feel heavy in their hand. Fibres in the fabric that most people wouldn't think can be itchy. The beds are bumpy. Food has textures you can't imagine. Like The Princess and the Pea, they can feel a pea under twenty mattresses.

15. They Are Disorganized: Piles are their favourite method of organizing. Once a task is complete, papers related to it are placed in a pile, where they stay until the piles grow too high. That's when the person with ADD becomes overwhelmed, frustrated, and cleans up. People with ADD have to be careful not to become hoarders. It's hard for a person with ADD to keep things in order because their brain doesn't function in an orderly manner.

16. They Need Space To Pace: When talking on the phone or having a conversation, people with ADD think better when they are in motion. Movement is calming and brings clarity to their thoughts.

17. They Avoid Tasks: Making decisions or completing tasks on time is a struggle. Not because they are lazy or irresponsible, but because their minds are full of options and possibilities. Choosing one can be problematic. It's easy to avoid making decisions because they are over-thinkers. They obsess and dwell in the depths of their minds.

18. They Can't Remember Simple Tasks: Another paradoxical trait of ADD is memory. People with ADD can't remember to pick up their clothes at the cleaners, milk at the grocery store, or appointments. On the other hand, they remember every comment, quote, and phone number they heard during the day. No matter how many post-its or calendar reminders they set, their distracted mind is always elsewhere. Visible items are easier to remember. That's why they have fifteen windows open on their desktop.

19. They Have Many Tasks Going On Simultaneously: Due to the constant activity in their mind, once a task is finished, they are ready to move on to the next job without closing up the prior study. The more going on at once, the better. Multi-tasking is one of their favourite activities.

20. They Are Passionate About Everything They Do: The emotions, thoughts, words, and touch of a person with ADD are powerful. Everything is magnified. This is a blessing when channelled properly. When a person with ADD does something, they do it with their heart and soul. They give it all they've got. They are intense, perceptive, and deep. This quality is what makes the person with ADD so lovable.

A person with ADD/ADHD has trouble controlling their impulses. They also have many excellent qualities that you will enjoy once you understand how they think and feel. Compassion, empathy, and patience will carry you through the most challenging times. It's essential to take extra care of yourself; take alone time regularly, do what you enjoy, find a support group, a therapist, a compassionate, wise friend, take frequent vacations, meditate, find hobbies and your passion. Most of all, learn how to breathe.

Managing Money And ADHD

Managing finances can be a challenge for people with ADHD. The symptoms of procrastination, disorganization, and impulsivity can create problems with finances. The following fact sheets provide strategies, tips, and resources that can help with successful money management:

- Managing Money and ADHD: Expenses and Goals
- Managing Money and ADHD: Saving and Spending
- Managing Money and ADHD: Money Management Schedule
- Managing Money and ADHD: Minding Your Debts

Curb Impulse Spending

We've all been guilty of impulse spending a last-minute decision to buy something that stood out in a store display or something more significant that we decided was worth the splurge. An impulse purchase may be small, like a pack of gum, or large, like a laptop. For an adult with ADHD, keeping impulse spending in check can be challenging, but your savings account and budget will thank you for taking the time to learn how.

Don't Know Where To Begin? Here Are A Few Tips For Curbing Impulse Spending:

- Identify your temptations and how to stay away from them. Where are you most likely to spend money on impulse? Examples of problem areas include malls, arts and crafts and other speciality shows, and online retailers.
- Shop with a list and stick to it. Before you go to any store, make a list of everything you want to buy and commit to it. If it helps, share the information with your spouse, partner, or friend before going, and then report back later.
- Add up your purchases as you shop. This will help you keep track of how much you're spending in real-time.
- Wait a set number of hours (24 is a good number) before making a big purchase. If you still want the item after that time passes and you have the money, you can decide to buy it.
- Unsubscribe from retail email lists. All those marketing emails are designed to get you to go to companies' websites and spend money.
- Find fun hobbies or things to do that are free or inexpensive. Explore neighbourhood museums and libraries, attend lectures, join support groups or clubs, visit public parks, start an exercise routine, or join an adult sports league in your area.
- Make it harder to spend your money. Think about leaving your credit and debit cards and chequebook at home, or only bring the minimum amount of money you'll need.

Manage Credit Cards And Debt

Credit card debt can quickly add up and take you in the wrong financial direction, especially if you don't pay off the bills. Balances build-up from interest, late payment fees, and over-the-limit charges, turning small purchases into huge expenses. Paying only the minimum amount due on significant credit card debt means it could take 30 years to pay off the entire balance. If you are someone who doesn't or can't pay off credit card balances each month, pause the next time you're thinking about charging something. Ask yourself if you love the item enough to spend the next 30 years paying for it.

Remember, Credit Cards Are Easy To Use, But They:

- Promote impulse spending;
- Make it hard to save money; and
- Make it easy for you to spend more money than when you pay with cash.

If credit card debt is a problem, consider storing your credit cards in a safe location at home, so they aren't an option when you're out shopping. If you're doing all your spending online or have trouble leaving the cards at home, think about using the trick of putting your credit cards in a container filled with water and freezing them. By the time you've defrosted the credit card, the urge to make the purchase may well have melted along with the ice. Or maybe it's time to take a good look at your credit cards and think about cancelling all but one, to have on hand in case of emergency.

Other Ideas To Cut Back On Excessive Credit Card Use Include:

- Have a trusted friend or loved one hold your card. If you decide to make a purchase, you will need to have a conversation about what you want to buy before giving you your card back.
- Immediately after purchasing with the credit card, write a check to your credit card company or bank for the purchase amount. That way, you know you're not spending more money than you have.
- Put a small sticker on your credit card that shows something you are saving for or part of your savings plan. It will remind you of your longer-term goals and force you to pause and ask yourself if the purchase fits in with those goals.
- Success with finances demands the elimination of debt and the prevention of new debt. If you tend to carry large balances on your credit cards, you may be better off not using credit cards. Think about meeting with a financial advisor to plan the best way forward for your financial situation. You may also want to consult a therapist to work on any emotional issues you have around money.

Managing Money And ADHD: Saving And Spending

Having savings is one of the best things you can do for yourself, your family, and your future. Maybe you'll need it to pay for an emergency, or perhaps it'll go toward the down payment on a new house, but knowing that you have some money saved can give you absolute peace of mind.

If you don't have any savings, start small and be patient with yourself as you learn this new habit. You might want to open a special bank account just for salvation or for one particular goal if it's a big one and has direct deposits automatically taken out of your paycheck. You might even choose not to have a savings debit card to make sure you have to think twice before spending money from this account.

Motivate yourself by making saving money fun and visual. For instance, you could make a chart with a savings "thermometer" and mark it as you hold, or create a bar graph on your computer and track your savings daily or weekly. For short-term savings, you might try putting cash in a special jar or an envelope with a photo of whatever you are saving for glued to the outside, just as a place to hold it until you can get it to the bank. That way, every time you put money in the envelope, you'll be reminded of what you're working toward.

Develop A Spending Plan

A spending plan or budget can help you prepare for many of the expenses you will have in a month or year. Since most utilities (electricity, phone, gas, water) and loan instalments are paid every month, you'll probably find it most helpful to construct a monthly plan. Some people call this "spending it before you get it," which means that when you get a paycheck, you already know how much of it you need for your expenses, and you will be less likely to spend it on a whim.

First, you need to figure out how much money you need each month write that amount down so you can see it. A spreadsheet can help develop this kind of spending plan.

Find what works for you in creating a budget. Here are some suggestions as you get started:

- Make a master list of all your expected expenses. Pull together amounts from purchases you made during the last 12 months. Use your chequebook records as well as bank and credit card statements.
- Use money management programs such as Quicken or Mint to gather all this information. You may also find an Excel spreadsheet helpful.
- Add up all the expenses from the past 12 months and divide by 12 to get your total average monthly payments.

Next, Think About Your Spending Plan Or Budget And How You Will Stick To It. Here Are A Few Suggestions:

1. Weekly Review: Choose a day of the week to be your regular day to review your spending plan and budget. Determine which bills or expenses you expect for the coming week. Then look at the entire month to determine which costs will need to be paid in the coming weeks. Pay all bills due that week. What if you need to wait for a deposit before you have enough money to cover all the due bills? You can write the checks and make a note reminding you to mail them once the money has been deposited. If you pay the bills online, schedule the day you know the money will be there.

2. Consider Making Payments Electronically: Most companies, such as utilities, car and mortgage lenders, rental agents, and credit card companies, have automatic bill payment systems that can make regular withdrawals from your bank account, so you don't even have to worry about getting payments in on time. Be sure you have enough money in your bank account to cover scheduled costs.

3. Savings Account: Open a savings account and make regular deposits to cover sudden emergencies and save for particular items or events. Cars break down, pets and children get sick, and homes need repairs or maintenance. By planning with your savings account, you'll be ready for them. You'll also want to save for non-emergencies or special events that might include clothing, concert tickets, and vacations. If you have direct deposit, you can have a set amount deposited into a savings account regularly or set aside an amount from every paycheck or once a month, depending on your situation.

4. Financial Calendar: It is helpful to have a visual reminder of your bills. An electronic or paper calendar that lists all incoming money and dates of expected payments such as rent or mortgage, utilities, insurance, credit cards, groceries, and fuel will help keep expenses on time.

5. Money Management Timeline: Some people find it helpful to organize money management ideas into a timeline that shows financial tasks and the amount of time it might take to accomplish each one. You can make your timeline to fit your goals and lifestyle.

6. Apps To Help With Money Management: There are many saving and spending apps and programs available for you to use on your smartphone or computer. Many of them are free. You might want to try out a couple and see which one works best for your needs.

Managing Money And ADHD: Money Management Schedule

Creating A Timeline

Some people find it helpful to organize money management into a timeline that shows financial tasks and how often they need to be done. It also helps to note how long you think each task will take. Sometimes, seeing that who can complete money management tasks quickly or don't have to be done can help motivate people to accomplish some or all of them. You can make your timeline to fit your goals and lifestyle. This is one example of what a timeline might look like.

Every Day

- Collect receipts that are in your wallet, car, desk drawer, or other location. (5 minutes)
- Enter receipts and expenditures in your finance software (Quicken, Mint, You Need a Budget, etc.) or chequebook and store the tickets in an envelope until the end of the month. (5 minutes)
- Open bills came in the mail and wrote on the envelope the date each one needs to be mailed. Put them in order of the date you have to pay them. Keep all your bills somewhere you will see them often, making sure the date you have to pay each one is visible. (5 minutes)

Once A Week

- Pay bills, write "PAID" and the date you paid each one on the part of the bill you keep; put that in your paid bills folder. As you file each statement, find the last paid invoice for that same account (the past month's electric bill, for example), remove it from the folder, and discard or shred it. (10 minutes)

- Look through your email or apps for notification of any automatic bill payments made from your account that week and enter them in your finance software or chequebook. (10 minutes)
- Review any expenses for the week that just ended, as well as any you expect in the coming week. (5 minutes)
- Visit your bank to deposit any checks and withdraw money for the week, if needed. If your bank has a mobile app, you may be able to save time by depositing checks from home, just by taking photos of the front and back once you've signed each one. (time depends on the distance to your bank)
- Review weekly spending, especially in any problem categories (areas where you have a history of saving or spending difficulties). (10-15 minutes)

Once A Month

- Balance your bank statement, either in your chequebook or online. This means comparing how much your bank says you spent and deposited into your account with your records. It's essential to balance your budget in case either you or the bank made a mistake. It also gives you a chance to refresh your memory as to your spending habits. (20 minutes)

- After you've balanced your bank account, discard or shred ATM receipts, debit receipts, and other receipts from the period covered by the most recent bank statement. (10 minutes)
- Look over your budget and compare your goals to your actual spending and saving. (15 minutes)
- Look for patterns that you are spending too much in certain areas (clothing, dining out, buying music online), so you can work to change that spending in the next month or two. (15 minutes)

Once A Year

- Collect your financial papers for tax filing—ideally, you'll keep everything in a folder throughout the year. This should include any tax forms you receive in the mail from your employer, bank, mortgage lender, investment firms, college or university, etc., as well as records of any charitable donations. (20 minutes)
- File your taxes or bring your information to a tax preparer. If you file your taxes yourself, you might want to use software to guide you through the process and help you find ways to get a (bigger) tax refund. The amount of time this takes depends on whether you complete your taxes yourself.

- After you've filed your taxes, organize your information, including a copy of your tax forms and related paperwork. Store it in a labelled box or large envelope; you should keep your taxes for seven years. (20 minutes)
- Look over your spending and saving for the past year and make an honest assessment of how you met your goals. (30-45 minutes)
- List significant expenses you may be facing in the coming year, such as buying a new car, sending a child to college, making home repairs or related purchases, or travel and vacations, so you can start saving for them. (30 minutes)
- Make a list of ongoing debts (home, car, school, medical), including how much you still owe and when you expect to pay each one-off. It's essential to keep track of your debts, so you can track your progress in paying them down. (30-45 minutes)

Managing Money And ADHD: Expenses And Goals

Managing finances can be challenging when you have ADHD, but it's an essential skill. You may find you're able to master it once you come up with your financial plan. Think how nice it would feel to be organized: You don't have to fear your bank account getting unexpectedly low, or that you'll be turned down for a loan, or that who will cut your power because you forgot to pay the bill.

Your Relationship With Money

For adults with ADHD, issues with the following things may make keeping up with financial matters more complex:

- Keeping track of bank balances or expenses
- Organizing checks, bills, and significant tax papers and avoiding late payments
- Spending and large credit card balances
- Avoiding or procrastinating on paying bills or organizing files
- Saving for future needs or wants

Know Where Your Money Is Going

Keeping a record of what you buy can help curb impulsive spending. It also allows you to see where your money is going. Carry a small notebook or find a smartphone app that works for you, and record all of your purchases, even small ones. Be sure to include what you buy or pay for online as well. When you track your spending, you'll see specific categories emerge. Those might have groceries, meals out, snacks, coffee shops, books, movies, gasoline, bus fare, clothing, newspapers, cosmetics, household items, donations, and hobbies.

You may find tracking your spending hard or annoying at first, but keep at it, even if just for a week or two. If you're married or in a partnership, your spouse or partner should keep track of their expenses, too, so you can compare notes. If you're single, you might ask a trusted friend or family member to check in with you to be sure you are keeping track. Even if you do not own a perfect record of every expense, the information you collect will help you improve your money management habits. Include both fixed and variable costs in your tracking.

Fixed expenses: housing, utilities, loans, transportation

Variable costs: food, gas, clothing, entertainment (an average amount or range)

Be sure to include monthly, quarterly, and yearly expenses such as taxes, homeowner association fees, and memberships.

Add up your fixed and variable expenses. If they total more than your income, you will have to take another look to see where you can save or cut things out. What's left over after those expenses is your disposable income. What you do with your disposable income will depend on your situation and your lifestyle preferences. You may use it for going out to dinner, making home repairs or improvements, taking vacations, taking a class, saving for retirement, and so on.

Think About Your Values And Goals

Take some time to reflect on your short- and long-term goals. If you have a spouse or partner, you should discuss your plans with them.

You might find it helpful to write notes or create a collage that shows a few things you'd like to save for. Sort your list or pictures into two groups: the essential (must-have for health, security, or well-being) and the nonessential (would like to have). What are the top three to five things on your list of essentials? Your list of nonessentials? What is coming between where you are now and where you would like to see yourself? Once you clarify your vision and identify any problem areas, you can set some money-related savings or spending goals.

Short-term goals might include:

- Saving a certain amount per week.
- Eating out less often to save money.
- Keeping your financial papers organized.

Mid-term goals might include saving for a vacation or a new piece of furniture or paying off a small debt like a store charge card.

Long-term goals might include saving for college tuition or planning for retirement.

Break down your goals into small action steps that you can take daily, weekly, monthly, or yearly. Don't be afraid to ask for help from a friend, a therapist, or a coach if you need it. Remember that successful money management means paying attention to all of your goals. They are an essential part of your money management routine.

CHAPTER 11: ADHD AND ORGANIZATION

ADHD And Organizing Your Space

Humorous though it may seem, disorganization can plague your soul and wreak havoc in your life. Disorganization is especially pronounced in people with Attention Deficit Hyperactivity Disorder (ADHD.) People with ADHD have trouble organizing things. They have problems managing time, their thoughts, and data.

Adults with ADHD tend to "organize" by putting things into piles that, over time, grow and increase like weeds. Whether in the workplace or at home, living in such a chaotic environment is like having cobwebs in the brain. Fortunately, some valuable devices and new habits you can employ to restore a measure of order and clarity.

Because the ADHD brain is low on filing cabinets, you need to set up more filing cabinets outside the brain. In other words, you need to replace the piles with files. You need to establish some structure in your daily life that will allow you to make up for what's missing internally in your mind.

Daily Living Tips For Adult ADHD

1. Check Your Planner 3 Times A Day: Whether you have ADHD or just too much to remember, organizing tips can help you manage your time and activities better. Get into the habit of putting all your appointments and activities on a calendar. It doesn't matter if it's a day planner, a smartphone app, or just a plain old desk calendar. Keep it in one spot and check it at least three times a day. Make it a habit to study at the exact times each day.

2. Make A New "To Do" List Every Day: Each morning, make a list of the things you want to get done that day. Try to keep your list realistic, so you'll have a good chance of getting to everything. Arrange your tasks in order of importance, putting the most important tasks first. Assign each task a specific time of day. Cross off each task when you complete it.

Start Organizing One Room At A Time

- Don't be intimidated by the idea of "getting organized." Start by putting things back where they belong and throwing away things you don't need.
- Tackle one room at a time starts with the easiest. Divide the room into sections if you need to.
- Schedule organization time in your planner. Use a timer to manage your work sessions.
- Ask yourself whether you want to keep items or toss them. If you're not sure, put them in a separate box to go through later.

Make Organization A Daily Habit

Don't think of it as cleaning up. Think of it as following your organization plan:

- If you keep items, they should have a home. Use filing cabinets, labels, clear storage boxes, and over-the-door organizers.
- Take 10 minutes each day to pick up and return items to their proper places.
- If you take it out, put it back.
- Keep a box for loose papers and other mislaid items to be put away. Go through it at the end of every day.

1. Keep Small Items Together: Place a small table or bookshelf near the entryway of your home. Put a tray or basket on top to hold essential items such as keys, wallets, watches, glasses, and phones. You can also use this area to have other things you want to remember, such as lunchboxes, briefcases, essential papers, or outgoing mail.

2. Have A Rotating Menu: Planning regular meals for the entire family may be a challenge. Create a "Top 10" dinner list or regular rotating menu of dishes that you can cook quickly. Try to keep those ingredients on hand, or list the ingredients on index cards you can take with you. Don't carry the burden of feeding everyone yourself: Have a floating "free" night when you order takeout, or share the kitchen responsibilities with other family members.

3. Follow A Mail Routine: Develop a system for checking and sorting mail every day. One idea is to create a particular area to hold all important mail, such as bills, insurance information, checks, and bank statements. Review this pile at least once a week, sorting tabs into a fortune to be paid and filing other important documents where they belong. Stop junk mail from coming to your house by taking your name off mailing lists.

4. Write Down What You Spend: Managing money can be difficult for people with ADHD, especially if you tend to make impulse purchases. Carry a notebook or use an electronic device or financial website to keep track of everything you buy, even minimal investments. Knowing how much you spend each month and what will help you manage your money.

5. Use Electronic Reminders: Forgetting meetings, deadlines, medications, or other responsibilities can create problems at work and in your personal life. For help, turn to computer programs and other electronic devices to remind you of appointments and deadlines. For example, set your computer or smartphone to alert you five minutes before every event in your calendar.

6. Tune Out Distractions At Work: Distractions at work can be a big challenge for adults with ADHD. Try these strategies:

- Route your calls to voicemail, then check it only at set times during the day.
- Ask for a quiet cubicle or office at work so you aren't distracted by others.
- Use a "white noise" machine or listen to earphones to drown out other sounds at work.
- Stick to doing just one task at a time.
- **Fight Boredom:** Many people with ADHD get bored quickly, especially during routine tasks or paperwork. This can make it challenging to stay focused at work. Try these tips:
- Break up big tasks into smaller tasks.
- Between tasks, take a walk or get fresh air.
- Take notes in meetings.

7. Simplify Your Life With Fewer Tasks: Organizing and simplifying your surroundings will help you reduce clutter, keep track of your belongings, and remove some of the distractions that prevent you from focusing.

8. Get More Exercise: Regular exercise may help manage your ADHD symptoms. At the very least, it can help you channel extra energy. But regular exercise and team sports can also help you work together with others, learn to set and meet goals and feel better about yourself. Some research suggests that physical activity may stimulate parts of the brain associated with ADHD. Activities like yoga and karate may be better for ADHD because they offer opportunities for memorizing movements.

Start Tasks With 15-Minute Blocks

When you're having trouble starting a project, try this exercise:

- Set a timer for 15 minutes.
- For those 15 minutes, focus on that one task only.
- When the time is up, decide if you can keep going for another 15 minutes.
- If you can, reset the timer. Keep going at 15-minute intervals for as long as you can.
- If you can't do anymore, stop and try again later or the next day.

Use Color Coding

Coloured files, folders, and notes can help you stay better organized. Here are a few examples:

- Use colour-coded files to keep track of different expenses, such as groceries, auto, entertainment, and utilities.
- Use different coloured pens or highlighting in your planner to separate work, personal, and family commitments.

- **Learn From Your To-Do Lists:** If you see many unfinished tasks left on your "to-do" lists, try to figure out why. Did you try to get everything done at one time? Did you list big tasks that could have broken down into smaller ones? Or did distractions keep you from completing your assignments? Use this information to help arrange future "to-do" lists or find ways to work more efficiently.

Organizing The Home And Office Space

Getting and staying organized is a real challenge for individuals diagnosed with ADHD. Many adults may have difficulties with clutter in both the home and the office and feel overwhelmed or stuck. Getting organized can help you in many ways, including:

- Increasing productivity
- Freeing up time spent looking for things
- Reducing anxiety
- Serving as a positive role model for your children
- Making more money by being efficient
- Improving your marriage, partnership, and other close relationships

Home organization is a skill that anyone can learn at any time. I honestly believe that. It's just easier for some than for others. I do not have ADHD, but I have successfully parented, taught, and professionally organized people who do. And along the way, I learned a lot about how the ADHD brain works.

ADHD is a spectrum disorder that manifests through the eight administrative processes of the brain:

- Flexible thinking
- Working memory
- Self-monitoring
- Task initiation
- Planning
- Organization
- Impulse control
- And emotional control.

The executive functions of the brain help you plan, organize, and complete tasks. If you have ADHD and are trying to organize your home, you are likely struggling with one (or more) of these executive functions, which makes home organization especially challenging. Challenging, but not impossible. These tips will help you change your mindset about what an organized home should look like and encourage you to get started.

Strategies To Get You Motivated And Keep You Going

One of the hardest things to do when making a change is getting started. Positive reinforcements or rewards can help motivate you to become more organized. Before you start an organizing task, select a prize to give yourself when you've finished. When you've completed the job, make sure you reward yourself.

You are getting a friend to help you make the job easier and go faster, especially if you need to declutter. Friends can help you get rid of things because they do not have the same sentimental attachment to them that you have. Online chat groups can also provide you with mutual support. Some have features where you make specific commitments to organize a space, move away from your computer to arrange for a while, and finally return to their computers to encourage each other.

The use of a timer and music can help you. Who can set the timer to go off in 15-minute increments, with pauses in between? Some people find it helpful to put on a favourite music playlist, begin organizing and keep working until the playlist finishes.

An Effective Strategy For Getting Organized

The best approach to learning a complex task is to break it down into smaller steps and tackle these steps one at a time. Organizing a physical space can be broken down into the following steps:

- Select the areas to be organized
- Put them in order from easiest to most difficult
- Start with the most straightforward space
- Schedule time to work on it
- Decide on the reward or motivation to encourage the completion of each step
- Divide the room into sections

- Work on one team at a time, sorting, discarding, or re-organizing each object in that section until it is finished

When the most accessible area is organized, gradually move up to the most difficult, repeating steps as needed.

1. Select A Space And Estimate/Schedule Time

The first step is to list all the physical spaces that need organizing, numbering the spaces from "easiest to organize" to "most difficult to organize," using higher numbers for more challenging locations. You can post a copy of this list on a bulletin board or refrigerator door, somewhere you can see it all the time. Start with the most straightforward space to maximize the chances of success, and later move on to the more challenging locations.

Select the most straightforward space from your list. Estimate how long it might take you to organize it. Pick a deadline to complete organizing this space. If the estimate is off, who can add additional time later? Divide the estimated time into several short work sessions 30 to 60 minutes each. If you believe you would get frustrated or bored in 30 to 60 minutes, shorten the session to 10 to 15 minutes and schedule more sessions. The idea is to start working for a short enough time that you can experience success without becoming frustrated and overwhelmed. Using a calendar, schedule enough short organizing sessions over the next few days or weeks to complete the task, adjusting your estimate if needed.

Record your deadline and the organizing times in the day planner.

2. Divide Your Selected Space Into Sections Or Centres

Divide the area you are working on into a grid and work on one portion of the grid at a time. There are several ways to divide the space:

Quartering: Divide the room into quarters visually or by marking it off with masking tape or string.

Around the Clock:

1. Divide the room into workable sections by dividing it like a clock.

2. Stand in the doorway of the room, make that spot noon and organize it first.

3. Work your way around the room systematically, organizing the area at 1:00, 2:00, 3:00, and so on until you return to where you started. If doing the entire room this way is too much, tackle one or two "hours" of the clock during each of your scheduled organizing sessions.

Zones: Organize the sections of the room by function. Keep all of the equipment, supplies, paperwork, and other items for a given position in that zone of the room. For example, to organize your home office, ask yourself what procedures might be accomplished in the office. Perhaps you decide that who will perform the following activities in the home office:

- Reading and responding to email
- Surfing the internet and making purchases online
- Paying the bills, doing the income taxes, and completing other miscellaneous financial paperwork
- Writing professional papers and reading scientific journals
- Putting photos and slides in albums and working on digital pictures on the computer

Who Could Organize The Room Into Four Zones?

1. Computer Zone: Computer on a desk, printer, modem, printer and computer supplies, shopping catalogues, scientific journals, and storage for professional papers

2. Photo Area: Camera, film, lenses, photo accessories, binders for negatives and slides, and photo albums

3. Financial Paperwork Area: File cabinets with financial records, bills, extra checks, bank books, and calculator

4. Reading Zone: A comfortable lounge chair with an overhanging lamp, a table by the side of the chair, and bookcases with books

3. Systematically Work On Each Section

Gather everything you need to do the job (such as several boxes, plastic containers, garbage bags, masking tape, markers, pencil and paper, cleaning supplies, labels). Set your timer or start the music you've selected. Start with three boxes and a trash bag. Title the boxes "keep here," "goes somewhere else", or "not sure." Place any leftover food and empty food containers in the trash bag. Place any dirty dishes or silverware in the "goes somewhere else" box to return to the kitchen when you are done.

Pick up one item at a time. Decide which box the item belongs in and determine whether the article is still helpful to you. If it's not, put it in the garbage bag. Put saved items either in the "keep here" box, if they belong in the section, you are now organizing, or in the "goes somewhere else" box if they belong in another department or room.

Don't take a lot of time with each item. If you cannot decide quickly to keep or discard the item, place it in the "not sure" box. Continue going through things until everything in the section has been sorted, or the timer has gone off, or the playlist has ended. Then, stop the project for the day. Take out to the trash. Take the "goes somewhere else" box and return those items to their "home." Don't worry that who may not yet organize the homes for these items; leave them in that section or room for now.

Leave the "not sure" box in the room until you have finished sorting all the items. Then, close and seal the box with masking tape. Write with a marker a future date three to six months away on the outside of the box. This is the date when you will re-open the box and review the contents. Mark the re-open date in your day planner. Place the container in a storage area. When you check the items on the designated day, make one of the following choices:

If you have not had to look for the item in that box during the three to six months storage time, then you don't need it. Put it in the trash or give it away.

If you have looked for the item or decide now to keep it, find a home and place it there. At the end of each organizing session, congratulate yourself on your successful effort and give yourself the reward you picked.

4. Finish Organizing The Space

Repeat the steps for organizing each section until you have finished the space. Congratulate yourself and treat yourself to an enormous reward. Move on to the next item on the list of areas to be organized and follow the above steps. Continue to follow these steps until all of the rooms on the list have been collected.

Tips For Staying Organized

After working very hard to organize the virtual spaces in your life, you want to keep them organized. Here are some tips and strategies to help you maintain the decluttered spaces.

- Paper ideas
- Four things to do with paper:
- Trash or recycle it
- Refer it to someone else
- Act on it now
- Save or file it

You can also reduce the need to deal with paper in the future by removing your name from mailing lists. Catalogue Choice is a website that you can use to unsubscribe from multiple catalogue mailing lists, and retailers have agreed to honour these requests.

Another way to reduce paper is to use your camera, scanner, or phone to take pictures of recipes, memos, newspaper clippings, or other documents that you want to save but don't need to have the originals of; save these on your computer and back up the files regularly. You can use computer folders to organize these images for easy access and searching. Once you scan the paper, recycle it.

Make A Ticker Filing System.

Every day your home or office is bombarded with papers, notes, phone messages, flyers, coupons, bills, and mail that you have to know about. The ticker system is a dated filing system that eliminates the piles, files, and lists that clutter up your life. The system consists of 43 folders, one marked for each month (labelled January–December) and one kept for each day of the month (labelled 1–31).

Put the current month folder in front of the 1–31 numbered folders. Keep these folders in plain sight (such as a folder stand on the desk or kitchen counter). File these papers in the folder of the date that you need to act upon them. To make this system work, always remember to check the folders daily.

At the end of each month, move the next month's folder to the front and sort the items inside that folder into the appropriate daily numbered files.

Storage Strategies

Try some of the following techniques for neatly storing items and maintaining organization:

- If you don't put things away because you are afraid you will never find them, try storing them in clear containers. Being able to see inside the container will also save time.
- Use over-the-door hanging organizers with divided pouches in each room to store things, such as office supplies, jewellery, makeup, tapes or CDs, cleaning supplies, pantry items, baby care items, gloves, hats, and scarves craft supplies.

- Store small items in under-the-bed boxes with lids.
- Purchase a tall trash can to store extra sheets and blankets or out-of-season clothes. Place the can next to your bed, cover it with a floor-length tablecloth, and use it as a nightstand.

The Launchpad

You can spend less time hunting for stuff by setting up a table or small bookshelf by your front door for items you need when you leave your home. Place a small container or basket on the table to hold keys, glasses, and wallets. Who can also place briefcases and backpacks there for the following day?

Centres

Set up centres to hold similar items and supplies needed to complete a particular task. Who can place the items for each centre in any available mobile container, including baskets, tackle boxes, buckets, and carts on wheels? This will save time because all of the supplies needed to complete a project will be in one place. Make a list of the centres that you develop and the items in each centre. Post the list on your bulletin board, so you will easily remember where these items are.

Eight Ways To Maintain A Newly Organized Space

1. The Handy Box

Keep a box or basket handy for items out of place as you clean out a room. When you come across out-of-place items, put them in the container. After cleaning the room, take a few minutes to put these items in the proper space.

2. At The Moment

- When you pass an open drawer, close it.
- When you pass a full wastebasket, empty it.
- When you see a clothing item on the floor, hang it up.
- When you see some loose papers, put them in the to-file box.

3. 10-Minute Pick-Up Pick-Up

Spend 10 minutes each night on a quick pick-up. Take a basket and go through the house, quickly picking up and dropping things off where they belong. Better yet, get the whole family involved by having them clean up their space each evening before bed.

4. Quick Clean

- Pick up the dropped stuff.
- Put away what you use.
- Wipe up a spill as soon as it happens.

5. Just For 15 Minutes

- This is an excellent way to get started on a project you have been putting off.
- Set a timer for 15 minutes.
- Focus your effort on one thing for those 15 minutes.
- When the timer goes off, decide whether you can keep going for another 15 minutes.
- If you can, set the timer again for the next 15 minutes.
- If you can't, simply stop and do the same thing later in the day or the next day until the project you are trying to finish is completed.
- It may seem like a short amount of time, but it soon makes a difference. You can always see and feel what has been accomplished in those 15 minutes.

6. Subtract Before You Add

Make a rule for yourself, "Always subtract before you add!" You will not add (purchase) a new item unless you subtract one (such as no new books or magazines unless you read or give away unread books or magazines).

7. Put It In Place

Whenever there are a few minutes to spare, put away five or ten items that are not in their correct place. These could be toys that the kids have left somewhere, letters that need filing away, or socks that need to be put in the drawer.

8. Toss/Donate Box

Keep a box or bag in a storage area to collect items to donate. As you notice an item, you don't want or use, immediately take it to the donate box. Don't let unwanted or unused items take up valuable space waiting for a periodic dig-out. Place small items in the trash and larger ones in a storage area for trash pick-up day.

CHAPTER 12: TIME MANAGEMENT

Good time management is tricky. It requires planning, executive function, self-discipline, focus, and resilience. Time management may feel like a slippery, foreign concept, but it comes down to the tug of war between maximizing the present or maximizing the future. The siren song of the current will always call sweetly, so apply some intentional effort to keep those future goals front and centre. Managing ADHD mainly involves helping the future to win over the present. Use these ADHD-tested strategies to increase productivity and get more done each day.

Practical Ways For ADHD Brains To See Time

1. For your morning routine, post a note in the bathroom stating the time you need to leave the bathroom. Put a similar note in your bedroom and another in the kitchen. Make sure there is a visible clock in each room.

2. When putting appointments into your schedule, including travel time before and after and prep or transition time. Then set the alarm to go off when that first step begins.

3. Take a couple of minutes at the start of your day to plan your priorities and when you will work on them.

4. Put your lights and TV on a timer to shut off to remind you to go to bed.

5. Use Internet-limiting devices, like Circle, to limit time online.

6. Turn off auto-play on your various streaming services so you see the current time between videos.

Practical Ways To Be Mindful Of Time

1. Schedule frequent check-ins with your boss or coworkers so you can't procrastinate.

2. Create external accountability by telling someone else what you intend to get done, then asking him to check in with you.

3. Create intermediate deadlines for your big projects (finish writing the report by Sunday, the first draft by Wednesday).

4. Make sleep, diet, and exercise a priority since these will give you more energy and allow you to use your time well.

5. Create rewards for completing tasks (you can go out after you finish the dishes).

6. Have a set bedtime so that you feel pressure to get things done earlier in the evening.

7. If delaying is costing you financially (in late fees, etc.), imagine what you can do with the money you will save by acting sooner.

Time Management Tips For Adults With ADHD

Attention deficit hyperactivity disorder (ADHD) often struggles with everyday tasks and getting things done promptly. For instance, a job that would be otherwise easy to complete in an hour takes three days instead. Do you often find yourself distracted until the time is wasted? The challenges of ADHD and attention deficit disorder (ADD) are genuine. But there is hope. When you understand how ADHD has affected all areas of your life, you can learn to minimize its impact and live successfully with ADD /ADHD.

Here are some steps to help you build confidence, clarify and prioritize your goals, minimize your ADHD challenges, and get you past being stuck to following through with your plans.

- Plan
- Check-in periodically during the day.
- Use a planning system
- Concentrate
- Take breaks
- Reduce clutter
- Avoid perfectionism
- Learn to say no
- Don't procrastinate
- Delegate

Challenge: Planning Too Many Activities

How many times have you committed yourself too much? Grossman says that this over-scheduling occurs relatively often. Sometimes we become too gung-ho or unrealistic about the number of things we can get done in a given period. Other times, we may have difficulty saying "no" to requests others make of us. Unfortunately, over-committing and over-planning simply set us up for frustration.

Solutions:

- Choose a planner that works for you, considering size, technology, ease of use, portability, colour, and feel.
- Mark out times for known, set, key events such as work times, meal times, carpools, and standing appointments.
- Keep note of items you "should" do versus things you "want" to do. You may want to tackle your disorganized filing cabinet, but you should first tackle an assignment that's due tomorrow.
- Create a to-do list and then choose no more than three to five high-priority items to complete on a given day, marking them with an asterisk or colour-coding system. Write those items in your planner in the gaps of time available.
- Think "subtract" or "swap" when you add an item to your daily plan. Keep in mind the finite number of minutes in a day and that you are only one person. If you have the means, consider delegating some tasks to others, like sending dirty clothes to the laundromat rather than doing the laundry yourself.

- If a big project overwhelms you, consider breaking it down into multiple mini-projects, with a deadline for each.

Challenge: Having What You Need To Get Out The Door On Time

It's time to go, but your necessary items are scattered all around the house. Where are those car keys? Where are my glasses?

Solutions:

- Establish holding places near the door for keys, wallets, backpacks, and purses. Make it a habit of placing those items in a particular area any time you walk in the door.
- Put any items you need to take with you in the morning in the designated holding place or on the floor next to the door. Encourage all family members to do the same.

Challenge: Having Too Much To Do In The Morning

You can't decide what to wear. Your shirt is wrinkled, so you have to iron it. You finally decide what to wear, but now one of your shoes is missing from the closet.

Solutions:

- Reduce morning stress by preparing the evening before. Gather all items for your morning outfit, including shoes and accessories, before you go to bed.

- Establish and post a list of the morning routine. Do only those items. Do not squeeze in anything else.

Challenge: A Lack Of Internal Cues That Help You Judge The Passing Of Time

How many times have you been engrossed in an activity on the computer and lost track of time? This happens to people with ADHD quite frequently. We get involved in an exciting exercise and ultimately lose our sense of time, and as a result, we miss an important meeting or pick the kids up from school on time.

Solutions:

- Strategically set timers to ring or vibrate as a convenient external cue of elapsed time. You may even use a combination of a vibrating watch alarm set as a warning signal and a freestanding timer set 15 minutes later as a reminder to get off the computer promptly.
- Set a cell phone or watch alarm to vibrate every 10 or 15 minutes. When the alarm goes off, use that as a cue to orient yourself in time. Ask yourself if you are doing what's most important at this moment and if you are where you need to be.

Challenge: Estimating How Long Specific Tasks Take

Grossman notes that with a fluid ADHD-style time sense, it is difficult to know if there's enough time to finish a report the morning before the big meeting, to take one last phone call before leaving to drop off the children at soccer practice, or to make "just one-stop" en route to the doctor's office in time for the appointment.

Solutions:

- Double or even triple the amount of time you think it will take to do something and then plan accordingly.
- Make a rule for yourself that you will simply not do that "one last thing" before leaving the house for an appointment or en route to a destination. Set and stick to your deadlines and to-do list.
- Hone your time sense by practising. Start by estimating how long tasks will take. Write your estimates in your planner next to the item and keep track of the actual time spent. Look for patterns. Do you usually underestimate how long it takes to drive places? Do you tend to overestimate how long it will take you to complete your expense report? With a vigilant practice of guessing and recording the actual elapsed time, the gap between your estimated and real-time will narrow. You'll feel more in control and will arrive at places consistently on time.
- Determine how much time it truly takes you to get ready to leave the house in the morning, accounting for everything that you must do.

Challenge: Failure To Account For Time Eaters

What are time eaters? Grossman explains that time eaters are the seemingly trivial, peripheral activities that accompany most actions we take, eating into our time without our awareness. They include traffic snarls, searching for parking spots, walking from parking lots into buildings, elevator delays, finding the right office, and the need to run back to the car for a forgotten item. Time eaters also show up at our workplace, interfering with on-task effectiveness. They include phone calls, audible email alerts, and stoppers-by.

Solutions:

- Build in plenty of time to account for time eaters. Double or triple the amount of buffer time you typically allow for travelling to a destination.
- To optimize timely task completion, choose a chunk of time when you'll turn off the phone ringer and your email alerts, and hang a sign on your closed door requesting no interruptions.

Challenge: A Desire To Avoid Being Early, Which Results In Being Late

Grossman notes that some people simply don't like to arrive at places early. They may dread the discomfort or tedium of waiting for a meeting or appointment to start.

Solutions:

- Pack a "guilty pleasures" tote bag and keep it in your car to use just in case you arrive somewhere early. Guity pleasure items are those you enjoy but often deny yourself due to a perceived lack of time. They might include magazines, novels, catalogues, or crossword and sudoku puzzles. A variation on this theme is a "found time" tote bag, which might consist of projects without a set deadline, such as thank-you cards (along with pens and envelopes). You may even find yourself aiming to arrive early so you can reward yourself with your "indulgent" activity.
- Use the wait as necessary downtime in your day. Try a simple meditation technique of focusing on your breath, or remind yourself that a few minutes of daily rest is required for recharging your brain, making it a productive use of your time.
- Take advantage of this time by accomplishing those things you're unlikely to schedule, such as cleaning out your wallet or purse, balancing your chequebook, or tweaking your to-do list.

CHAPTER 13: ADHD IN WOMEN

Women And Girls

Knowledge of ADHD in women is minimal as few studies have been conducted on this population. Women have only recently begun to be diagnosed and treated for ADHD. Today, most of what we know about this population is based on the clinical experience of mental health professionals who have specialized in treating women.

Impact Of ADHD In Women

ADHD in young girls is often overlooked, the reasons for which remain unclear, and many females are not diagnosed until they are adults. Frequently, a woman comes to recognize her ADHD after one of her children has received a diagnosis. As she learns more about ADHD, she begins to see many similar patterns in herself.

Some women seek treatment for ADHD because their lives are out of control, their finances may be in chaos; their paperwork and record-keeping are often poorly managed; they may struggle unsuccessfully to keep up with the demands of their jobs; and they may feel even less able to keep up with the daily tasks of meals, laundry, and life management. Other women are more successful in hiding their ADHD, struggling valiantly to keep up with increasingly tricky demands by working into the night and spending their free time trying to "get organized." But whether a woman's life is clearly in chaos or whether she can hide her struggles, she often describes herself as feeling overwhelmed and exhausted.

While research of ADHD in women continues to lag in adult males, many clinicians are finding significant concerns and coexisting conditions in women with ADHD. Compulsive overeating, alcohol abuse, and chronic sleep deprivation may be present in women with ADHD.

Women with ADHD often experience dysphoria (unpleasant mood), major depression, and anxiety disorders, with rates of depressive and anxiety disorders similar to those in men with ADHD. However, women with ADHD appear to experience more psychological distress and have a lower self-image than men with ADHD.

Compared to women without ADHD, women diagnosed with ADHD in adulthood are more likely to have depressive symptoms, are more stressed and anxious, have a more external locus of control (tendency to attribute success and difficulties to external factors such as chance), have lower self-esteem and are engaged more in coping strategies that are emotion-oriented (use self-protective measures to reduce stress) than task-oriented (take action to solve problems).

Studies show that ADHD in a family member causes stress for the entire family. However, stress levels may be higher for women than men because they bear more responsibility for the home and children. In addition, recent research suggests that husbands of women with ADHD are less tolerant of their spouse's ADHD patterns than wives of men with ADHD. Chronic stress takes its toll on women with ADHD, affecting them both physically and psychologically. Women who suffer chronic stress like that associated with ADHD are more at risk for diseases related to chronic stress, such as fibromyalgia.

Thus, it is becoming increasingly clear that the lack of appropriate identification and treatment of ADHD in women is a significant public health concern.

The Challenge Of Receiving Appropriate Treatment

ADHD is a condition that affects multiple aspects of mood, cognitive abilities, behaviours, and daily life. Effective treatment for ADHD in adult women may involve a multimodal approach that includes medication, psychotherapy, stress management, and ADHD coaching and professional organizing.

Even those women fortunate enough to receive an accurate ADHD diagnosis often face the subsequent challenge of finding a professional who can provide appropriate treatment. Very few clinicians are experienced in treating adult ADHD, and even fewer are familiar with the unique issues faced by women with

ADHD. As a result, most clinicians use standard psychotherapeutic approaches. Although these approaches can help provide insight into emotional and interpersonal problems, they do not support a woman with ADHD learn to manage her ADHD better daily or learn strategies to lead a more productive and satisfying life.

ADHD-focused therapies are being developed to address a broad range of issues, including self-esteem, interpersonal and family issues, daily health habits, daily stress levels, and life management skills. Such interventions are often referred to as "neurocognitive psychotherapy," which combines cognitive behaviour therapy with cognitive rehabilitation techniques. Cognitive behaviour therapy focuses on the psychological issues of ADHD (for example, self-esteem, self-acceptance, self-blame) while the cognitive rehabilitation approach focuses on life management skills for improving cognitive functions (remembering, reasoning, understanding, problem-solving, evaluating, and using judgment), learning compensatory strategies, and restructuring the environment.

Medication Management In Women With ADHD

Medication issues are often more complicated for women with ADHD than for men. Any medication approach needs to consider all aspects of the woman's life, including coexisting conditions. Women with ADHD are more likely to suffer from coexisting anxiety and depression and a range of other states, including learning disabilities. Since alcohol and drug use disorders are common in women with ADHD and may be present early, a careful history of substance use is essential.

Who may further complicate medication by hormone fluctuations across the menstrual cycle and the lifespan (e.g., puberty, perimenopause, and menopause) with an increase in ADHD symptoms whenever estrogen levels fall. In some cases, hormone replacement may need to be integrated into the medication regimen used to treat ADHD.

Other Treatment Approaches

Women with ADHD may benefit from one or more of the following treatment approaches:

1. Parent Training: In most families, the primary parent is the mother. Mothers are expected to be the household and family manager roles that require focus, organization, planning, and the ability to juggle multiple responsibilities. ADHD, however, typically interferes with these abilities, making the job of a mother much more difficult for women with ADHD.

Furthermore, because ADHD is hereditary, a woman with ADHD is more likely than a woman without the disorder to have a child with ADHD, further increasing her parenting challenges. Women may need training in parenting and household management geared toward adults with ADHD. The evidence-based parent management programs effective in children with ADHD are also recommended for parents with ADHD. However, research on these parent training approaches has indicated that parent training may be less effective if the mother has high ADHD symptoms. Thus, it may be necessary to incorporate adult ADHD life management strategies into parent training programs for mothers with ADHD.

2. Group Therapy: Social problems for females with ADHD develop early and appear to increase with age. Women with ADHD have more significant self-esteem problems than men with ADHD and often feel shame when comparing themselves to women without ADHD. Because many women with ADHD feel shame and rejection, psychotherapy groups specifically designed for women with ADHD may provide a therapeutic experience, a place where they can feel understood and accepted by other women, and a safe place to begin their journey toward getting themselves more and learning to manage their lives better.

3. ADHD Coaching: ADHD coaching, a new profession, has developed in response to some adults with ADHD for structure, support and focus. Coaching often takes place by telephone or email.

4. Professional Organizing: As contemporary lives have become increasingly complicated, the organizer profession has grown to meet the demand. Women with ADHD typically struggle with very high levels of disorganization in many areas of their lives. Some women can maintain organization at work but at the expense of an organized home. For others, disorganization is widespread, which increases the challenges and difficulties of ADHD. A professional organizer can provide hands-on assistance in sorting, discarding, filing, and storing items in a home or office, helping to set up systems that are easier to maintain.

5. Career Guidance: Just as women with ADHD may need specific guidance as a parent with ADHD, they may also greatly benefit from career guidance, which can help them take advantage of their strengths and minimize the impact of ADHD on workplace performance.

Many professional and office jobs involve the same tasks and responsibilities most challenging for a person with ADHD, including paying attention to detail, scheduling, paperwork, and maintaining an organized workspace. Sometimes, a career or job change is necessary to reduce the intense daily stress experienced by most individuals with ADHD. A career counsellor who is familiar with ADHD can provide precious guidance.

Ways That Women With ADHD Can Help Themselves

It is helpful for a woman with ADHD to work initially with a professional to develop better life and stress management strategies. However, the following methods can be used at home, without the guidance of a therapist, coach, or organizer to reduce the impact of ADHD:

- Understand and accept your ADHD challenges instead of judging and blaming yourself.
- Identify the sources of stress in your daily life and systematically make life changes to lower your stress level.
- Simplify your life.
- Seek structure and support from family and friends.
- Get expert parenting advice.
- Create an ADHD-friendly family that cooperates and supports one another.
- Schedule daily time-outs for yourself.
- Develop healthy self-care habits, such as getting adequate sleep and exercise and having good nutrition.
- Focus on the things you love.

Individuals with ADHD have different needs and challenges, depending on their gender, age, and environment. Unrecognized and untreated, ADHD may have substantial mental health and education implications. Women with ADHD must receive an accurate diagnosis that addresses both symptoms and other vital issues with functioning and impairment, which will help determine appropriate treatment and strategies for the individual woman with ADHD.

Personality Strengths Of People With ADHD

Not every person with ADHD has the same personality traits, but some personal strengths can be advantageous, not a drawback.

Examples Of These Traits Include:

They are energetic: Some individuals with ADHD often have seemingly endless amounts of energy to channel toward success on the playing field, school, or work.

1. **I Was Spontaneous:** Some people with ADHD can turn impulsivity into spontaneity. They may be the life of the party or maybe more open and willing to try new things and break free from the status quo.

2. **They Are Creative And Inventive:** Living with ADHD may give the person a different perspective on life and encourage them to approach tasks and situations with a thoughtful eye. As a result, some with ADHD may be inventive thinkers. Other words to describe them may be original, artistic, and creative.

3. **They Are Hyperfocused:** Some people with ADHD may become hyperfocused, according to research. This makes them so intently focused on a task that they may not even notice the world around them. The benefit to this is that, when given an assignment, a person with ADHD may work at it until its completion without breaking concentration.

Sometimes a person with ADHD needs assistance in harnessing these traits to their benefit. Teachers, counsellors, therapists, and parents can all play a role. They can help a person with ADHD explore a creative side or devote energy to finishing a task.

Things To Love About ADHD!

- The Undeniable Power of ADHD
- The Drive of ADHD Hyperfocus
- Real ADHD Resilience
- A Sparkling Personality
- ADD Generosity
- Ingenuity
- A Strong Sense of Fairness
- Willingness to Take a Risk
- Spontaneity
- A Great Sense of Humor!
- Constant Surprises
- Last of the Romantics
- Engaging Conversational Skills
- Compassion
- Persistence
- Superstar Creativity
- A Different Perspective
- Contagious Motivation
- Being Punctual and Highly Organized

Postmenopausal Women With ADHD

Is It ADHD Or Menopause?

You're "of a certain age," and suddenly your memory has so many holes you call it "swiss-cheese brain." You lose things more frequently, and your get lost in your thoughts, distracted in a heartbeat. Women diagnosed with attention deficit hyperactivity disorder (ADHD) sometimes panic, worrying about their worsening symptoms. Women who have not yet been diagnosed with ADHD who experience these occasionally debilitating symptoms ask their doctor, "What's happening? Do I have ADHD ... or Alzheimer's?"

Regardless of whether you have ADHD or not, menopause influences everything! After "the change," women's estrogen levels drop about 65 per cent, which affects the uptake of dopamine and other neurotransmitters. Less estrogen means lower dopamine and serotonin levels, causing the onset of ADHD-like symptoms: increased difficulty concentrating, memory dysfunction and cognitive problems, and less mental clarity. If you have ADHD, the further decrease of dopamine from your already-low levels means that existing symptoms worsen and new ones pop up.

Are These Symptoms Of Menopause Or ADHD?

Some women who have had undiagnosed ADHD all of their lives find that worsening symptoms send them to their doctor's office looking for answers. But ADHD-like symptoms do not always indicate the presence of the condition. If you have only recently developed symptoms (and haven't been present since childhood), menopause is probably the culprit. Talk with your doctor about symptom relief.

If you've been diagnosed with ADHD, menopause's effects on the condition often require treatment adjustments. Work with your doctor to increase medication dosage or to try an extended-release med, get more exercise (which can sharpen focus and, in the process, reduce the odds of developing osteoporosis), and consider hormone therapy. For many women, the best course of treatment is estrogen, for three to four months, followed by ten days of progesterone.

Complicating matters is the fact that about 85 per cent of women experience some sexual dysfunction after menopause. When you could use humour and support from your partner to cope with "swiss-cheese brain," you may find that your relationship becomes more strained.

Treat Your Symptoms

It is essential, at every stage of your life, to keep ADHD symptoms under control. This may mean working with several professionals a psychologist, an internist, and a gynaecologist. Educate yourself about ADHD and what's going on with your body, keep lists of medications, and chart your symptoms. Doctors rarely consider hormonal fluctuations when developing a treatment plan.

If you have problems paying attention, getting organized and keeping your life on a steady keel, a professional may prescribe a stimulant, even in the absence of an ADHD diagnosis. But who should do this in the context of a comprehensive, multimodal plan that includes everything from nutritional changes and exercise to psychotherapy and hormone-replacement therapy? As for those problematic sexual changes, helping your partner understand that they are expected is a good place to start.

Perimenopause Problems: How Changing Hormones Exacerbate ADHD Symptoms In Women

Studies in women have shown that estrogen improves memory and cognitive functioning. Research using objective psychometric tests has reported higher scores for women taking estrogen. Estrogen appears to exert a global effect on cognition-enhancing or maintaining aspects of verbal memory but does not appear to have a similar impact on spatial memory.

In addition, it is now known that estrogen exerts profound effects on mood, mental states, and memory. Low levels of estrogen in women are associated with PMS, postnatal depression, and postmenopausal depression. It has been proposed that whenever brain estrogen falls below the "minimum brain estrogen" requirement, for whatever reason and at whatever age, brain dysfunction may result.

Women with ADHD need to be aware of several perimenopausal and menopausal issues. First, menopause comes with a whole host of symptoms, including memory problems and mood changes, in addition to hot flashes, insomnia, etc. Women entering menopause frequently complain of difficulty with short-term verbal memory, word retrieval, and mental clarity. These symptoms are now thought to relate to decreasing estrogen levels that affect the brain. As a woman with ADHD, you need to work with a physician aware of the interaction between ADHD symptoms and estrogen levels.

Perimenopause is also a time associated with mood changes and depression in some women who have had no previous history of the disorder. These women report feeling sad, irritable, tired, and worried and having difficulty sleeping. This depression and the cognitive deficits associated with decreasing levels of estrogen that occur as a woman enters menopause, combined with ADHD symptoms, may cause a woman with ADHD to have difficulty coping with her ADHD symptoms as well as she was previously.

She may find herself becoming less functional as she enters this phase of her life. I find this is often the reason why a woman seeks help for her ADHD for the first time in her late 30s, 40s, and 50s. At that time, she may present to a physician with full-blown ADHD or a worsening case if they have been diagnosed previously.

Physicians need to take all of this information into account and design a holistic approach to assist women with ADHD in getting back on a more even keel. Treating ADHD in women at the various life stages is a challenge, and no two women have the exact needs. Stimulant medication dosage may need to be increased, and most women need symptom coverage for 16 to 20 hours per day.

In addition, sleep issues need to be addressed. Multiple doses of long-acting stimulants depending on their duration are advisable, and the new non-stimulant product lasting 24 hours may need to be considered along with motivation.

Antidepressants and estrogen or thyroid hormone supplements may also be warranted in some instances.

Women should also practice good self-care, eating a wholesome, nutritious, well-balanced diet, and getting plenty of exercise and sleep. She should discuss her symptoms with a physician and discuss the possibility of taking vitamin supplements and using alternative therapies to boost estrogen or omega-3 fatty acids. Above all, a woman with ADHD should be kind to herself and get all of the help and support she can to make this difficult transition time more comfortable for her.

Treatment For Women With ADHD

Women face an additional challenge when treating their ADHD. Hormones! The natural fluctuations of hormones, both monthly and through the different phases of life, can increase ADHD symptoms. However, when you understand what is happening and why you feel empowered and more assertive, seek the best treatment for your ADHD.

ADHD, Estrogen, And The Brain

Estrogen is one of the main hormones that are responsible for regulating the female reproductive system. Estrogen also plays a role in cognitive functions as it is involved in the modulation of the neurotransmitters serotonin, dopamine, and norepinephrine. These neurotransmitters help with focus, concentration, mood, and memory. Estrogen levels vary considerably in the last two weeks of the menstrual cycle and during perimenopause and menopause.

When estrogen levels are low, you may experience increased feelings of irritability, moodiness, and depression, problems with sleep, anxiety, difficulty concentrating, fuzzy thinking, forgetfulness and memory issues, fatigue and loss of energy, as well as hot flashes.

Women with ADHD tend to be particularly sensitive to lower estrogen levels. ADHD itself is associated with a dysfunction in the neurotransmitter systems in the brain.

Hormones And ADHD Stimulants

Stimulant medications are either methylphenidate-based (e.g. Ritalin) or amphetamine-based (e.g. Adderall). Both classes block the reuptake of dopamine and norepinephrine, leading to higher available levels in the synapse (space between nerve cells).

In amphetamines they also increase the release from and then block the recycling process inside the cell. They also stop or slow down their speed of reabsorption. This means that the neurotransmitters stay in the neural synapse longer, allowing messages in the brain to be more effectively transmitted and received. As a result, your ADHD symptoms are reduced. Studies have found that estrogen may aid in the effectiveness of stimulants.

Conversely, lower estrogen levels are often associated with less effectiveness from or less response to stimulant medications. To complicate things further, the hormone progesterone may make stimulants less potent. Let's look at how estrogen levels change throughout your life.

Puberty

The onset of puberty is also associated with hormonal levels changes, so early adolescent girls with ADHD may experience increased difficulties managing ADHD symptoms. It is not unusual for girls to experience intense mood swings, irritability and become more over-reactive emotionally during the pubescent years.

Also, in their early teenage years, girls may start noticing that their ADHD medication is not as effective in helping them to manage their ADHD symptoms. This may be because, during puberty, both estrogen and progesterone levels increase. While estrogen seems to aid in the effectiveness of stimulants, progesterone likely decreases it.

PMS

There are fluctuations in estrogen and progesterone levels during the monthly menstrual cycle, and there tend to be varying response rates to stimulant medications. It is helpful to track your symptoms by keeping a log or simple journal, noting when symptoms seem to escalate during your cycle. This way, you and your doctor will have a clearer picture of the specific patterns you are experiencing. You can work to develop coping strategies to minimize any negative impact.

Pregnancy

Many women report that ADHD symptoms decrease during pregnancy, as estrogen levels tend to be much higher. However, not every woman experiences a decrease in ADHD symptoms. In addition, doctors often advise women to stop taking their ADHD medication during pregnancy, which means pregnancy can be challenging as you are managing ADHD symptoms without medication.

Postpartum

After the baby is born, estrogen levels drop, and ADHD symptoms return (or persist). Postpartum depression is something that can appear for new ADHD moms, mainly if depression was a condition that coexisted with ADHD before pregnancy.

The lack of sleep that comes with a new baby and the stress of creating a new routine can make ADHD symptoms worse. If you are breastfeeding, it is essential to get advice from your doctor before taking ADHD medication.

Perimenopause And ADHD

Perimenopause often begins when a woman is in her late 30s or early 40s. It is the transition phase where a woman moves out of her reproductive years and into menopause. During this time, estrogen levels can fluctuate. You may notice that ADHD symptoms appear to be getting worse. A change in ADHD medication dosage can be helpful. Also, speak with your doctor if you feel depressed or anxious, as these conditions can also appear at this time.

Menopause And ADHD

Menopause typically occurs between the ages of 45 and 55, with the average age at approximately 51. With the onset of menopause, there is a significant drop in estrogen levels for most women. However, many women say that once they reach menopause, they feel better than they did during perimenopause because their estrogen levels have stabilized.

Career Advice For People With ADHD: How To Keep The Job You Love

Many experts say that getting on the proper medication is the most critical factor in succeeding in a career if you have ADHD. While this is important, there are additional strategies that you can implement to be more effective at work. As discussed above, picking a job that is a good fit for you is also essential. Boredom can be a problem for people experiencing ADHD, so finding a job that keeps you interested and engaged could help you retain your focus at work. Once you have found that job, these 11 additional tips could help you enjoy your work and achieve success with more ease:

1. Assess Your Strengths And Weaknesses: This can not only help you pick a job that is a better fit for you but also help you customize your work environment so that you can work more effectively. For example, if sitting at your desk for long periods makes you too restless, then consider approaching your boss about getting a standing desk.

2. Minimize External Distractions: Do you have a time of day that you can focus better? Are you more focused when things are quiet? If you can have some flexibility in your scheduling, then talk to your boss and see if you can adjust your hours to work during your best times or when the office is quieter. You can also minimize the potential for interruptions by setting times when you let your phone go to voicemail, reducing the clutter on your desk, turning your desk toward a wall rather than the door, and letting your coworkers know that if your door is closed, it means that you do not want to be interrupted.

3. Minimize Internal Distractions: Sometimes good ideas will pop into your head that is not related to the task you are working on. Instead of spending your time thinking about them, quickly jot them down for later review and then move on.

4. Implement A Planning System: Organize and manage everything that you need to do on a given day. This includes phone calls that you need to make, emails that you need to send, meetings that you need to attend, and projects and reports that you need to work on. Prioritize these activities and then spend your day working from your list. Only vary from it if something comes up that is genuinely urgent. Keeping your day structured can be the key to staying on task.

5. Create Checklists For Tasks That Have Many Steps: If you are working through a task or project with many steps to it, then create a quick list that you can use as you go. It can help you stay focused and ensure that you are not missing essential steps.

6. Track Your Time: If one of your symptoms is hyper-focus, then you may have trouble completing your work in a timely fashion because you get too involved in it and lose track of time. Try setting alarms or reminders on your computer that pop up to keep you aware of how much time you are spending and when you should be moving on to something else.

7. Get Moving: If hyperactivity is one of your symptoms, then take every opportunity that you possibly can to move. Walk around while you talk on the phone, walk to your coworkers' or boss' offices when you need to speak to them, take a break from your desk every hour to walk around, or even spend five minutes doing some quick, simple exercises at your desk.

8. Give Yourself Extra Time: Whether it's getting to work, going to appointments, or scheduling meetings, always give yourself spare time, if possible. And when you are getting ready to go, avoid the impulse to do one more thing. Write it down for later and get on your way. This can help you arrive for work, appointments, and meetings on time.

9. Avoid Procrastination: Stop waiting for the right moment; just dive in and get started. And avoid negative self-talk. Think positively instead. Post inspirational and positive messages around your work area. Instead of thinking, "I am never going to get this done today," think, "I have two hours to get halfway through this project." Focus on one step at a time so that you don't get overwhelmed by the project as a whole.

10. Keep Your Desk, And Office Organized: Having a cluttered or disorganized work environment can lead to distraction. So if you are done with something, then don't save it.

Either shred or file items as you go. Always have file folders and labels ready. And keep a three-hole punch and binders handy for items that don't fit into file folders.

Best Jobs For Women With ADHD

Forget everything you've read about ADHD brains falling short on the job. We are not too disorganized, too distracted, or too bored to succeed at the workplace. As it turns out, most adults with ADHD are satisfied with their work and feel their current positions showcase and leverage their strengths. Sitting down and answering these questions can help you uncover what type of worker you are and what kind of work might be a good fit for you. As you consider these factors, you may want to know that, in general, the best work environments for people with ADHD tend to:

- Be fast-paced
- Have a high level of interaction
- Offer variety in daily routines
- Have ample problem-solving opportunities
- Encourage creativity
- Provide broadly focused jobs that draw upon knowledge from many areas

Top Careers For People With ADHD

- Cosmetology: Cosmetologist, Nail technician

- Business: Marketing specialist, Sales representative
- Creative Arts: Graphic designer, Journalist
- Culinary Arts: Chef, Restaurant manager
- Education: Early childhood educator,
- Teacher
- Healthcare: Nurse, Paramedic
- Legal & Criminal Justice: Police officer, Private investigator
- Skilled Trades: Auto mechanic, Truck driver
- Technology: Computer support technician, Network system administrator

Let Your Inspiration Guide You

Are you feeling inspired to go after a career that you will love? You can succeed in any profession as long as it interests you and falls in line with your strengths. So act on that motivation right now and see what types of programs are offered in your area. Just enter your zip code into the school finder at the top of the page to make your first move toward attaining one of the great jobs for people with ADHD!

Simple ADHD Concentration Tips

Whoever first said "focus on what's important" must not have had adult ADHD. From conversations with people you value most, such as family and friends, to essential tasks that will advance your career, it can seem almost impossible to stay concentrated when you have adult ADHD. You don't mean to zone out, but you do. ADHD makes it harder for your brain to focus on the details, so your mind wanders while others are speaking. This can be frustrating for you and them. But changing your health routine in simple ways can help you pay attention and become a better listener. Take a look at these tricks.

1. Take Deep Breaths: It may seem obvious, but you'd be surprised how many people forget this critical step when they're stressed out. Practising meditation and taking deep breaths can help improve your ability to focus, said Shane K. Perrault, PhD, a clinical psychologist and founder of the ADHD Performance Clinic in Greenbelt, Md. "When you have ADHD, your blood doesn't flow to the part of the brain where high-order decisions are made," he explained. Meditation and breathing exercises can help you relax and better manage your symptoms. "When you're relaxed, more blood flows to the brain and it functions better," Perrault said.

2. Eat Smart: If you think your food has more to do with your figure than your brain, think again. Have you ever heard of brain food? What you eat directly affects your energy level and your ability to focus. Following a healthy diet can help improve many of your ADHD symptoms, including your inability to concentrate, Perrault said. People with adult ADHD need to be sure to start the day with protein at breakfast if you begin to feel sluggish come mid-morning if you eat carbohydrates solely, and it's hard to concentrate when you're tired. Limit the number of sweets and processed foods you eat throughout the day. They are metabolized quickly, causing your blood sugar to spike. Then it drops just as quickly, causing you to have ADHD brain fog and lose concentration.

3. Jazz It Up: If you're having trouble concentrating because the task at hand is tedious, make it more exciting, said David Rosenberg, MD, professor and chief of child psychiatry and psychology at the Children's Hospital of Michigan and Wayne State University School of Medicine in Detroit. Approach it just like you would for your child: if you want him to clean up his messy room, you might have him imagine each object that needs to be put away like an aeroplane, Dr Rosenberg suggested, and then they "can find a good landing place on the shelf for each item." Adults with adult ADHD can use this same trick to make work tasks more appealing or finally get to that list of chores. While you're playing waste basketball with rotten food in the fridge, you're also teaching yourself how to focus.

4. Find Your Space: An essential strategy for staying focused when you have adult ADHD is to work in a space where there are few distractions. Ask your boss if you can move away from a TV or radio that's always on. Working in a noisy environment can worsen ADHD symptoms; ask for an office or cubicle that's away from others so that their conversations don't distract you. Another option is to use a white noise machine to save you from total silence, delighting some adults with ADHD more than loud noises.

5. Get Some Exercise: Like meditation and deep breathing, exercise stimulates brain function, essential to managing ADHD symptoms. Add regular exercise to your daily ADHD routine to get your heart pumping and your brain in gear. "People with ADHD have crazy energy," Perrault said. "When you exercise, it helps dissipate that energy, and when you return to work, you can function better, pay more attention, and focus on what you're doing."

6. Prioritize Your Tasks: It may seem so simple it sounds stupid, but keeping a to-do list can make a huge difference. Having multiple tasks ahead of you can be overwhelming when you have ADHD. Writing down each item in order of importance will help complete tasks that seem less daunting and help you to wrap your head around the next steps. Arrange lessons by highest to lowest preference and then tackle the list from top to bottom. Or, Rosenberg said, rank them by difficulty and do the simplest ones first to get them out of the way. You'll have a sense of accomplishment as you proceed, which can help you to manage your symptoms better and keep going.

7. Speak Up: If you're in a meeting at work and find you just can't concentrate any longer on what everyone is saying to you and each other, you may need a moment to refresh. Communicating your needs to others is key to developing a successful ADHD management strategy. You can't control your condition in a bubble. You may have to tell your coworkers or friends that you have adult ADHD. Explain that sometimes it's difficult for you to concentrate for extended periods and that getting some fresh air will help. When you return, you can continue the conversation. Take the time to educate your coworkers about adult ADHD so they will understand and appreciate your honesty.

Life-Management Tools For Women With ADHD

If you are a woman with ADHD, there are many things that you can do to reduce your ADHD challenges and to live a more satisfying life. While medication can be helpful as you work to make changes in your life, it won't make those changes for you. It may be beneficial to work with an ADHD specialist in solution-focused psychotherapy to get started on building a more ADHD-friendly life. Still, there are also many things that you can do with the help of friends, support groups, and greater self-knowledge.

Form Or Join A Women's ADHD Support Group

Often the biggest struggle is an internal one. Societal expectations have been deeply ingrained in many women. Breaking out of a mould of impossible expectations is easier with the support of others. Many women find support groups for women with ADHD a powerful source of encouragement and understanding. They work to develop more realistic expectations of themselves and develop better strategies for dealing with impossible situations.

Educate Significant Others About ADHD And How It Affects You

Husbands may feel anger and resentment toward an ill-kept house or misbehaving children, assuming that their wife "just doesn't care." Her parents may react judgmentally, questioning why their daughter's home is messy and why she may need more emotional, physical, or financial help than their non-ADHD children. Non-ADHD friends may intentionally or unintentionally give negative messages. Work to educate all of the "significant others" in your life about the impact of ADHD so that they can support you and help you to problem-solve instead of judging and blaming you. It's hard enough to be a woman with ADHD without being surrounded by family and friends who blame you for your difficulties.

Invite your spouse to a local adult ADHD support group. It is often an eye-opener to listen to other people with ADHD describe their challenges and their marriages. Your spouse may be more open to change when he hears other husbands tell their marriages and the strategies they have learned to live a calmer, better-managed life with their spouse.

It's "All In The Family"

Work to create an "ADHD-Friendly" environment in your home. Chances are, if you have ADHD, one or more of your children do as well. If you can approach your ADHD and that of other family members with acceptance and good humour, the frequency of emotional explosions will decrease, and you'll be able to save more energy for the positive side of things. Building an ADD-friendly home environment involves:

- We identify causes of chronic stress (such as over-commitment and chronic lateness) and reduce them.
- We are developing household routines to go to bed at night and get up in the morning to work more smoothly.
- Create "calm down spaces" for family members that are prone to emotional explosions when feeling stressed. A calm down space can be any quiet area that provides a comfortable place to lie down and contains calm-down objects such as a device for playing soft music, a snuggly blanket, and, for children, perhaps a stuffed toy.
- Become a family that problem-solves instead of blames.
- Learn to assign tasks according to strengths and preferences.
- De-clutter and organize your environment. Clutter and disorganization is not only a sign of stress but also a cause of stress.

- Consider working with an ADHD coach or professional organizer to get help in creating your ADHD-friendly home environment.

Simplify Your Life

Most women with ADHD are overbooked and overcommitted. Look for ways to reduce your commitments and those of your children. So many families today are chronically over-scheduled. Don't fear that you are depriving your child by not trying to keep up with the over-schedulers next door.

Get A Half-Hour Of Aerobic Exercise Every Day

You may cry, "Who has time for exercise?" but, as John Ratey, MD, and ADHD specialist writes, the most critical thing you can do to improve brain functioning (and reduce ADHD struggles) is aerobic exercise. You don't need to join a gym or spend money on expensive classes if you cannot. It may be easier to find a half-hour each day to exercise if you exercise at home. Create a routine. Exercise is most likely to happen if it occurs at a routine time and studies show that morning exercise is more likely to be consistent. As the day goes on, more and more events may interfere with the time you set aside for movement. Try it for a week, consistently, for a half-hour every morning. You'll find you are feeling better, focusing better, and sleeping better.

Don't Hang On To Friends That Criticize And Can't Understand Your Problems.

Look for friends that appreciate the best in you and do not judge you for your shortcomings. Joining a women's ADHD support group can be the beginning of finding this kind of friendship. Often, in a support group, women with ADHD report that it is the first time in their life that they have been in a group of women that truly understand and appreciate their struggles. Try to avoid putting yourself among women to stir up feelings of inadequacy due to their perfectionist expectations and unfavourable comparisons.

Build In "Time-Outs" Daily

Time-outs are essential as stress reducers. Married women with ADHD should ask their husbands to commit to specific blocks of time on the weekend to take full responsibility for the children. If possible, single-parent mothers with ADHD should try to arrange for a regular babysitter several times a week and reserve these times to do something restful! If you are a single woman with ADHD, make sure you don't overbook yourself leave time for doing anything.

Don't Place Yourself In Burnout.

One mother of two ADHD children, who was doing a great job of parenting her children, was also able to recognize her limitations. She arranged for summer sleep away camp for a month each summer with two such challenging children. She also set for brief visits, one at a time, to grandparents. This allowed her to spend time with each son without his having to compete with his brother. Try to recognize feelings of overwhelm before you're completely burnt out and look for ways to give yourself a break.

Burnout isn't only the province of mothers. If you are a single working woman with ADHD, you may need to guard against spending too many hours at the office and neglecting self-care. Many single career women with ADHD work hard to manage ADHD patterns at work but neglect their home life entirely. Or overcommitment to outside activities. Single women need to consciously make time to "do nothing," to relax and regenerate.

Eliminate And Delegate

Women with ADHD need to learn to eliminate and delegate activities in their daily lives to create more balance. The organizational tasks of life are more challenging if you are a woman with ADHD. Spending more on household help may be one of the best investments you can make in developing a more ADD-friendly, lower-stress lifestyle.

Specialized Parenting Classes

Women with ADHD who are the parent of a child with ADHD face a unique challenge. And if they are single parents, that challenge is even more significant. Children with ADHD are more challenging, need more structure and support, and often have special educational and psychological needs. If you have a child with ADHD, it's essential to seek consent and training in how to work with and help your child. ADHD provides "Parent to Parent" training groups that are highly affordable and can be extremely valuable, giving you parenting tools and the support and encouragement of other parents who understand the parenting challenges you face.

On the outside looking in, it may be easy for other parents to judge a woman with ADHD when her children misbehave. But what any parent of an ADHD child knows is that kids with ADHD don't respond the way non-ADHD kids do. As the mother of a child with ADHD, you have a challenging job. So don't blame yourself or allow others to judge you. Instead, focus on getting the training and support you need.

The Importance Of Focusing On The Things They Love

It is so easy to become caught up in focusing on the ADHD challenges that you never allow yourself to focus on your talents, your strengths, and on the things you love. As a woman with ADHD, your goal should be to understand and accept yourself. Try not to measure your success by someone else's yardstick. Instead, celebrate your ADHD gifts. So many women with ADHD are full of spontaneity, warmth, creativity, humour, sensitivity, and spirit.

As a woman with ADHD, work to create opportunities to be your best self and look for people who can appreciate the best in you.

Exercise Tips For Women With ADHD

Studies show that exercise can be just as effective as stimulant medications for treating ADHD. Activity triggers the brain to release dopamine and serotonin, which improves mood, reduces stress and anxiety, enhances working memory, executive function, impulse control, learning, and memory. However, for women with ADHD sticking to an exercise routine can be challenging, especially when it feels like a struggle to get through the day.

Below Are Seven Tips.

1. **Start Small:** Don't commit to working out seven days a week when you know from experience typically, two days is more realistic. Start with something so easy you can't say no. Celebrate your small accomplishments. Even taking a 20-minute walk around the block can help you get your mind right.

2. **Make Yourself A Priority:** Women with ADHD tend to be people-pleasers and put the needs of others first. Take care of yourself so you can be better for the people in your life. For new moms, even small workouts can go a long way for mental sanity. Make yourself a priority whenever possible.

3. **Find An Activity That Is Fun For YOU:** The best exercise is the activity that makes you feel the most energized and body positive. Let go of the pressure to do a specific type of workout because it is "ideal for weight loss", etc. If you have ADHD, you

know that trying harder or forcing yourself to do something doesn't work. If you hate running and prefer Bhangra Dancing, do you!

4. Mix It Up: Satisfy your natural curiosity and need to explore by experimenting and trying new things. One way to do this is ClassPass, an app that gives you access to thousands of different group fitness classes in your area, so you don't have to commit to one gym or studio.

5. Ditch Your Inner Critic: Women with ADHD tend to be hard on themselves. You may have a voice in your head saying, "I should be able to stick to a routine," "it shouldn't be this hard." Ditch your inner critic and forgive yourself if you're not sticking with something consistently. Let go of the all-or-nothing mindset and remember that every little bit counts. Perhaps it's parking four blocks further away from work. Or you are taking the stairs and having a pedometer and tracking steps. That can be something just straightforward visual to see.

6. Make It An Adventure: Women with ADHD are natural-born explorers. Harness this strength by turning exercise into an experience. Take a hike or explore a new area of your city by walking, biking, or running. Let your ADHD mind be stimulated by the colours, sights, and sounds around you.

7. On The Days When You Just Can't Even: Living with ADHD can be draining. If there are some days you just need to relax and rest, do it. Listen to your body; deep down, you always know what's best for you.

How Exercise Can Help Women With ADHD

You may have already heard that regular exercise can give your mood a boost. If you have ADHD, a workout does more than make you feel good. It can help control your symptoms, too. Even a single session of moving your body can make you more motivated for mental tasks, increase your brainpower, give you energy, and help you feel less confused. It acts on your brain in a lot of the same ways as your ADHD medication.

To reap these rewards, though, you need to exercise the right way and the right amount. The key is to find an activity that fits your lifestyle and then stick with it.

Get The Most Out Of Moving Around

The effects of exercise only last for so long, just like medicine. Think of your workout as a treatment "dose." Aim for at least one 30- to 40-minute activity a day, 4 or 5 days a week. The exercise you choose is up to you, but make sure it's "moderately intense," which means that during your workout:

- Your heart rate goes up
- You breathe harder and faster
- You sweat
- Your muscles feel tired

Talk to your doctor if you're unsure how intense your exercise should be. They may recommend you to use a heart rate monitor or some other device to make sure you get the most out of your workout.

Types Of Exercise You Can Do

Aerobic exercise. This is anything that gets your heart pounding. You want to do something that raises your heart rate and keeps it there for a set amount of time, like half an hour to 40 minutes. Aerobic exercise creates new pathways in your brain and floods it with the chemicals that help you pay attention.

You Can Try One Of These:

- Running
- Walking briskly
- Biking
- Swimming laps

You can do these activities outdoors or indoors, but if you have a choice, go outside. Studies show that being in nature while you move can reduce your ADHD symptoms even more than when you exercise inside.

Martial Arts: Experts say the more complex your exercise is, the better for your brain. Sports like karate, taekwondo, jiujitsu, and judo focus on self-control and bringing together your mind and body.

When You Do Martial Arts, You Get Training In Skills Like:

- Focus and concentration
- Balance
- Timing
- Memory
- Consequences of actions
- Fine motor skills

Other Complex Exercises: If martial arts isn't your thing, other physical activities that also challenge your mind and body are:

- Rock climbing
- Dance
- Gymnastics
- Yoga

Strength Training: If you're only just starting with exercise, go for aerobic activities like walking or jogging at first. After you've been at it for a while, add in some strength work for variety. Try exercises like:

- Lunges
- Squats
- Pushups
- Pullups

- Weightlifting

Team Sports: If you join a softball or soccer league, it may be just the thing to get you up and moving several times a week. Organized sports have all the benefits of physical exercise with the bonus of a social group to motivate you.

Teamwork hones your communication skills and helps you think through your actions and plan. Being part of a team can also improve your self-esteem.

How To Keep At It

Just like medicine, exercise only helps you treat ADHD if you keep it up. But if you have problems with attention span, how do you stay the course? Try these tips:

- **Keep It Interesting:** Switch up the type of exercise. You can stay out of a rut if you change your activity every day or week.
- **Find A Partner:** A workout buddy can help you stay on track and help pass the time while you sweat.
- **Move-In The Morning:** If it fits in your schedule, exercise first thing in the morning before you take your medication. That way, you'll get the most benefit from all the extra mood-boosting chemicals in your body.
- **Maintain Meds:** Exercise can give you a huge leg up on your ADHD symptoms, but it doesn't replace your

medication. Don't stop your other treatments unless your doctor says it's OK.

Exercise And The Brain

Exercise isn't just good for shedding fat and toning muscles. It can help keep the brain in better shape, too. When you exercise, your brain releases neurotransmitters, including dopamine, which help with attention and clear thinking. People with ADHD often have less dopamine than usual in their brains.

The stimulant medicines that are often used to treat adult ADHD work by increasing the availability of dopamine in the brain. So it makes sense that a workout can have many of the same effects as stimulant drugs.

Fitness can have the following benefits for adults with ADHD:

- Ease stress and anxiety.
- Improve impulse control and reduce compulsive behaviour.
- Enhance working memory.
- Improve executive function. That's the set of skills needed to plan, organize, and remember details.
- Increase levels of a brain-derived neurotrophic factor. That's a protein involved in learning and memory. It's in short supply in people with ADHD.

More Reasons To Exercise

Beyond helping with ADHD symptoms, exercise has several other benefits. Getting regular workouts can help you:

- Stay at a healthy weight. That's important because evidence suggests that people with ADHD are more likely to become obese.
- Reduce your risk of heart disease, diabetes, and certain types of cancer.
- Keep your blood pressure and cholesterol levels in a normal range.
- Strengthen your bones.
- Improve your mood and self-esteem.

How Often Should You Exercise?

Health experts recommend that you get at least 150 minutes of moderate-intensity exercise a week. That works out to about 30 minutes of fitness a day, five days a week.

If you're doing more intense aerobic workouts such as running or taking indoor cycling classes, you can get away with about 75 minutes of exercise a week.

How To Deal With Adult ADHD (Or ADD)

If you have attention deficit hyperactivity disorder (ADHD), previously known as ADD, everything from paying the bills on time to keeping up with work, family, and social demands can seem overwhelming. ADHD can present challenges for adults across all areas of life and can be tough on your health and both your personal and on-the-job relationships. Your symptoms may lead to extreme procrastination, trouble meeting deadlines, and impulsive behaviour. In addition, you may feel that friends and family don't understand what you're up against.

Fortunately, there are skills you can learn to help control your symptoms of ADHD. You can improve your daily habits, learn to recognize and use your strengths, and develop techniques that help you work more efficiently, maintain organization, and interact better with others. Part of helping yourself may also include educating others to help them understand what you're going through.

Change won't happen overnight, though. These ADHD self-help strategies require practice, patience, and, perhaps most importantly, a positive attitude. But by taking advantage of these techniques, you can become more productive, organized, and in control of your life and improve your sense of self-worth.

Tips For Getting Organized And Controlling Clutter

The hallmark traits of ADHD are inattention and distractibility, making organization perhaps the most significant challenge adults with the disorder face. If you have ADHD, the prospect of getting organized, whether it be at work or home, may leave you feeling overwhelmed.

However, you can learn to break tasks down into smaller steps and follow a systematic approach to organization. By implementing various structures and routines and taking advantage of daily planners and reminders, you can set yourself up to maintain organization and control clutter.

Develop Structure And Neat Habits And Keep Them Up

To organize a room, home, or office, start by categorizing your objects, deciding which are necessary and which can be stored or discarded. To manage yourself, get in the habit of taking notes and writing lists. Maintain your newly organized structure with regular, daily routines.

1. Create Space: Ask yourself what you need daily, and find storage bins or closets for things you don't. Designate specific areas for things like keys, bills, and other items that can be easily misplaced. Throw away stuff you don't need.

2. Use A Calendar App Or Day Planner: Effective use of a day planner or a calendar on your smartphone or computer can help you remember appointments and deadlines. With electronic calendars, you can also set up automatic reminders so scheduled events don't slip your mind.

3. Use Lists: Make use of lists and notes to keep track of regularly scheduled tasks, projects, deadlines, and appointments. If you decide to use a daily planner, keep all lists and notes inside it. You also have many options for use on your smartphone or computer. Search for “to do” apps or task managers.

4. Deal With It Now: You can avoid forgetfulness, clutter, and procrastination by filing papers, cleaning up messes, or returning phone calls immediately, not sometime in the future. If who can do a task in two minutes or less, do it on the spot, rather than putting it off for later.

Tips For Managing Your Time And Staying On Schedule

The trouble with time management is a common effect of ADHD. You may frequently lose track of time, miss deadlines, procrastinate, underestimate how much time you need for tasks, or find yourself doing things in the wrong order. Many adults with ADHD spend so much time on one charge, known as “hyper-focusing”, that nothing else gets done. These difficulties can leave you feeling frustrated and inept and make others impatient. But, there are solutions to help you better manage your time.

Time Management Tips

Adults with attention deficit disorder often have a different perception of how time passes. To align your sense of time with everyone else, use the oldest trick in the book: a clock.

1. Become A Clock-Watcher: Use a wristwatch or prominent wall or desk clock to help you keep track of time. When you start a task, make a note of the time by saying it aloud or writing it down.

2. Use Timers: Allot yourself limited time for each task and use a timer or alarm to alert you when your time is up. For longer assignments, consider setting the alarm to go off at regular intervals to keep you productive and aware of how much time is going by.

3. Give Yourself More Time Than You Think You Need: Adults with ADHD are notoriously bad at estimating how long it will take to do something. Every thirty minutes you think it will take you to get someplace or complete a task, give yourself a cushion by adding ten minutes.

4. Plan To Be Early And Set Up Reminders: Write down appointments for fifteen minutes earlier than they are. Set up reminders to ensure you leave on time and make sure you have everything you need ahead of time, so you're not frantically looking for your keys or phone when it's time to go.

Prioritization Tips

Because adults with ADHD often struggle with impulse control and jump from one subject to another, completing tasks can be difficult, and large projects can seem overwhelming. To overcome this:

- **Decide What To Tackle First:** Ask yourself what the essential task is that you need to accomplish, and then order your other priorities after that one.
- **Take Things One At A Time:** Break down large projects or jobs into smaller, manageable steps.
- **Stay On Task:** Avoid getting sidetracked by sticking to your schedule, using a timer to enforce it if necessary.

Tips For Managing Stress And Boosting Mood

Due to the impulsivity and disorganization that often accompany ADHD, you may struggle with erratic sleep, an unhealthy diet, or the effects of too little exercise, all issues that can lead to extra stress, bad moods, and feeling out of control. The best way to stop this cycle is to take charge of your lifestyle habits and create healthy new routines.

Eating well, getting plenty of sleep, and exercising regularly can help you stay calm, minimize mood swings, and fight any symptoms of anxiety and depression. Healthier habits can also reduce ADHD symptoms like inattention, hyperactivity, and distractibility, while regular routines can help your life feel more manageable.

Exercise And Spend Time Outdoors

Working out is perhaps the most positive and efficient way to reduce hyperactivity and inattention from ADHD. Exercise can relieve stress, boost your mood, and calm your mind, helping work off the excess energy and aggression that can get in the way of relationships and feeling stable.

- Exercise daily. Choose something vigorous and fun that you can stick with, like a team sport or working out with a friend.
- Increase stress relief by exercising outdoors, people with ADHD often benefit from sunshine and green surroundings.
- Try relaxing forms of exercise, such as mindful walking, yoga, or tai chi. In addition to relieving stress, they can teach you to control your attention and impulses better.

Get Plenty Of Sleep

Sleep deprivation can increase symptoms of adult ADHD, reducing your ability to cope with stress and maintain focus during the day. Simple changes to daytime habits go a long way toward ensuring solid nightly sleep.

- Avoid caffeine late in the day.
- Exercise vigorously and regularly, but not within an hour of bedtime.
- Create a predictable and quiet "bedtime" routine, including taking a hot shower or bath just before bed.
- Stick to a regular sleep-wake schedule, even on weekends.

Eat Healthfully

While unhealthy eating habits don't cause ADHD, a poor diet can exacerbate symptoms. By making simple changes in what and how you eat, you may experience significant reductions in distractibility, hyperactivity, and stress levels.

- Eat small meals throughout the day.
- Avoid sugar and junk food as much as possible.
- Make sure you include healthy protein at every meal.
- Aim for several servings of fibre-rich whole grains each day.

Practice Mindfulness

As well as reducing stress, regular mindfulness meditation can help you resist distractions, lower impulsivity better, improve your focus, and provide more control over your emotions. Since hyperactivity symptoms can make meditation a challenge for some adults with ADHD, starting slowly can help. Meditate for short periods and gradually increase your meditation time as you become more comfortable with the process and maintain focus. The key is to draw on these mindfulness techniques during your daily life to keep you on track. Experiment with free or inexpensive smartphone apps or online guided meditations.

How Can Mindfulness Help People With ADHD?

Unlike many ADHD treatments, mindfulness develops the individual's inner skills. It improves your ability to control your attention by helping to strengthen your ability to self-observe, train attention, and establish different relationships to stressful experiences. In other words, it teaches you to pay attention to paying attention and make people more aware of their emotional state so that they won't react impulsively.

Can I Learn To Practise Mindfulness On My Own?

Yes, the essential practice is straightforward. Just sit down in a comfortable place where you won't be disturbed and spend five minutes focusing on the sensation of breathing in and breathing out. Pay attention to how it feels when your stomach rises and falls. Soon, you may notice that you're thinking of something else, your job or some noise you just heard, or your plans for later in the day. Label these thoughts as "thinking," and refocus your attention on your breath.

Do this mental training daily. Every couple of weeks, increase the length of time you spend on the exercise by 10 minutes, 15, up to 20 or more if you feel you can. Try the same thing throughout each day, focusing on your breath for a few minutes as you walk from place to place, or when you're stopped at a red light or sitting at the computer.

You can practice mindfulness at any time, even during conversations with others. Turning on the mind-awareness state at any time during your day, even if only for a few minutes, is excellent training. It's essentially letting go of the busyness of your thinking and bringing your attention to what's happening in the present moment in everyday life.

Meditation For ADHD: Why And How Women Benefit

1. Meditation Is ADHD-Friendly

There are many ways to meditate, meaning there's a form out there that works best for your brain. Personalized mantras can be particularly effective, for example, for their simplicity. Rather than consciously focusing to quiet a busy or distracted mind, mantra meditation asks you to simply repeat a phrase in your head and let it carry you effortlessly to a place of calm and rest. The advantage of mantra meditation is that it affords little opportunity for the mind to wander, which is one of the biggest hurdles for newcomers and those who struggle the most with focus. This refocusing of the mind, if done regularly, can clear the mind and help you improve your focus.

2. Meditation Improves Communication Skills

Some women with ADHD struggle with impulsivity and hyperactivity, which manifests as a tendency to interrupt others or talk excessively. Alongside its calming and de-stressing qualities, meditation also helps improve communication skills over time by encouraging pauses and reflection. With improved verbal abilities, women are less likely to feel overwhelmed in conversations and social situations and more likely to find a happy middle ground when interacting with others.

3. Meditation Builds Coping Skills

Meditation enables your mind and body to enter a resting state far more profound than that in even your deepest point of sleep. Tapping into this state gives your nervous system (which is responsible for feelings of stress) a chance to relax deeply. The result is that cortisol levels and other stress hormones are reduced by up to a third, whilst production of our happy hormones is increased, making you much more resilient to unnecessary but inevitable future stress. This is particularly important for women with ADHD. It helps take away some of the fear and anxiety while building confidence and allowing them to be more accurate.

4. Meditation Is "Portable."

who can do meditation anywhere and at any time the individual needs it the most, making it the perfect, discrete tool for ADHD symptom management? While meditation is not a replacement for ADHD medication, it can form part of a comprehensive treatment plan and significantly improve the quality of life for women with ADHD.

Can Meditation Help With ADHD?

If you have ADHD, meditation might help you relieve some symptoms and generally feel better.

Meditation Can Improve:

- Attention
- Decision making
- Self-control
- Ability to switch between tasks
- Complex thought processes
- Working memory
- Anxiety and mood

Even if you're not keen on the idea of sitting still and clearing your mind, you can still meditate. Try to:

- Focus on yourself at the moment.
- Accept the thoughts that come to you without trying to change them.
- Relax the alertness of your body and mind.
- Use an "anchor" to help with focus, whether a sound, an object, or a repetitive physical movement.
- There's no cure for ADHD. But if you're looking to top up the care, you get from your doc, meditation may benefit.

Tips For Increasing Your Self-Esteem When You Have ADHD

You can do a lot to increase your self-esteem, and best of all, it is all under your control. You don't need to rely on other people.

1. Believe In Yourself

Repeated negative experiences and failures affect your self-esteem. This leads you to doubt your abilities and talents. To break the cycle and start improving your self-esteem, it is essential to start believing in yourself.

Believing in yourself might sound cliché, but it is a significant first step to improving your self-esteem if you can begin to trust your strengths and talents.

2. Focus On Your Strengths

We are all born with unique talents and strengths. What are yours? If you aren't sure, notice what tasks and activities are easy for you next week. Which ones do you enjoy doing, and which ones do you get compliments on? These are all clues!

Spending time noticing these things is a fast track to improving your self-esteem. Rather than trying to get good at tasks that are hard for you, spend the majority of your time doing things you are good at. Apply this rule to all areas of your life – work, home, hobbies, etc.

3. Develop Your Skills

In addition to focusing on your strengths, there are some basic skills you need to succeed in life and feel good about yourself. These skills might not come naturally to you because of how your ADHD brain works. However, it is possible to get good at them with time.

Learn How To Be Excellent:

- **Time Manager:** Arriving on time makes you feel reliable.
- **Money Manager:** Overspending or forgetting to pay your mortgage nibbles away at your self-esteem.
- **Meal Planner:** iI's hard to feel your best when you are hungry or eating junk food.
- **Housekeeper:** A dirty home full of clutter and funky smells erodes your self-esteem.

These tasks may be more challenging for you because they require skills that ADHD makes difficult. However, it is possible to become good at all of them.

4. Give Yourself Positive Feedback

How you were praised and disciplined as a child affects how you saw yourself and how you view yourself today. Children with ADHD can receive more criticism than praise. As a grown-up, you might focus on all the things you did "wrong" or didn't do well because that has become your default mode.

From now on, for every criticism you give yourself, acknowledge two things that went well. This will help rebalance things which will help improve your self-esteem.

5. **Don't Compare Yourself To Others.**

As a child, you may have been in the habit of comparing yourself to others. Your siblings, friends, and classmates probably could do things you found hard, like pay attention in class or sit still. When you measure yourself unfavourably with others, it lowers your self-esteem, as we rarely make comparisons where we fare better.

How Not To Speak To Someone With ADHD

Suppose you, your child, or your spouse/partner has attention-deficit/hyperactivity disorder (ADHD). In that case, you may encounter naysayers who simply do not understand the condition and its impact on everyday life.

Unfortunately, there are many misconceptions about ADHD, and these misunderstandings can be exceedingly hurtful to people living with it. Some people inaccurately believe ADHD is a "made up" disorder that is over-diagnosed and over-medicated. Others perceive ADHD as a benign, inconsequential condition easily managed with good parenting and disappear as a child moves into adulthood.

Whether you are the parent of a child with ADHD, the partner or spouse of someone with ADHD, or have ADHD yourself, you have likely heard some (or all) of the following faulty and provoking statements about the condition.

What Not To Say To Someone With ADHD

It's so important to understand what not to say so you can be as supportive as possible to those living with ADHD or those with loved ones living with ADHD. Here are some common phrases to avoid and why.

"ADHD Isn't Real. Why Don't We Just Let Kids Be Kids?"

This incorrect statement has to do with the validity of ADHD as an actual condition. Friends may innocently claim to have had an "ADD moment" or to have "a little bit of ADHD." You may hear people complain that "we don't let kids be kids anymore."

"Everybody Has A Little ADHD. It Isn't A Big Deal."

Indeed, everyone experiences occasions of forgetfulness and inattention. And what parent hasn't shared their child's behaviours veering out of control? These are everyday occurrences. For children and adults with ADHD, however, these are more than an occasional problem. For someone with ADHD, symptoms are present at such intensity that they significantly impair day-to-day life.

"ADHD Is Too Quickly And Too Frequently Diagnosed."

You may hear people say that "we are too quick to diagnose a child who is simply active and energetic." Yet, the parents of more than six million children between the ages of 2 and 17 who have been diagnosed with ADHD would likely disagree.

A proper ADHD diagnosis can be vital in getting help for your loved one. If left undiagnosed, ADHD can lead to academic, behavioural, emotional, social,

"People use ADHD as an excuse for bad behavior. They are just lazy and need to try harder."

Sometimes people make the inaccurate assumption that if a child or adult with ADHD would just "try harder," they could be more successful. This can lead the person with ADHD to be labelled in negative ways.

To add fuel to this fire, it is common for someone with ADHD to show fairly dramatic fluctuations and inconsistencies in their performance. It can be puzzling when someone can complete tasks quickly and correctly while performing these same tasks quite poorly.

This uneven pattern of productivity and accuracy is typical for someone with ADHD. It can be beyond frustrating for those who don't fully understand the impairments associated with the disorder. The truth is that people with ADHD exert a tremendous amount of energy and effort just trying to organize, focus, and keep themselves on track.

ADHD is never an excuse for behaviour, but it is often an explanation that can guide you toward strategies and interventions that can help better manage symptoms.

"ADHD Is Caused By Poor Parenting Or Lack Of Discipline."

Unfortunately, many parents of children with ADHD have to deal with these types of judgments around their parenting ability. It is simply not true that poor parenting or a lack of discipline leads to ADHD. Children with ADHD can indeed be much more challenging to parents. It's easy to become frustrated and doubt your parenting skills when you have a child with ADHD, mainly when these misperceptions around the causes of ADHD exist.

ADHD is a neurobiological condition that is primarily caused by genetics. Certainly, a person's environment can influence the expression of ADHD. Both children and adults with ADHD benefit from structure, routines, and behavioural interventions.

"Students With ADHD Who Receive Special Accommodations Have Unfair Advantages."

If ADHD affects learning and impairing academic performance in the classroom, a student may receive instructional support and accommodations. The purpose of such special accommodations is to ensure that the student's individual educational needs with disabilities are met as adequately as those students without disabilities. Rather than giving an unfair advantage to students with ADHD, special accommodations level the playing field.

"ADHD In Females Is Less Severe Than ADHD In Males."

It is a common misconception that girls and women with ADHD are less affected by their symptoms than males with ADHD. The fact is females with ADHD experience significant struggles that are often overlooked. Females with ADHD are often misdiagnosed as having depression, anxiety, or bipolar disorder.

Girls with unrecognized, untreated ADHD tend to internalize problems to a much greater degree. Research has also shown that some females with ADHD had an increased risk of cigarette smoking, overall lower self-esteem, and more self-injurious behaviours compared to their male counterparts.

Like undiagnosed males with ADHD, undiagnosed females are also at risk for chronic underachievement.

The difficulty mothers with ADHD face in coping with the demands of everyday life can easily overflow into parenting. Because of the genetic link to ADHD, many of these mothers will be parenting children with ADHD children who require even more in terms of organization, attention, and consistency.

CHAPTER 14: ADHD MYTHS AND FACTS

ADHD Myths And Facts

Myths

- There is no such medical condition as ADHD.
- ADHD is caused by bad parenting. All the child needs is good discipline.
- ADHD is a life sentence.
- Having ADHD means the person is lazy or dumb.
- The diagnosis of ADHD is confirmed if certain medicines (psychostimulants) have a positive effect on what seem to be symptoms of ADHD.
- Medicine for ADHD will make a person seem drugged.
- Medicine prescriptions for ADHD have significantly increased in the past few years because the condition is being overdiagnosed.
- Psychostimulants are no longer valid after puberty.
- Children with ADHD are learning to use the condition as an excuse for their behaviour.
- Children outgrow ADHD.
- If a child has ADHD, they can always be diagnosed in the doctor's office.

Fact

- ADHD is a medical disorder, not a condition of the child's will. A child with ADHD does not choose to misbehave.
- ADHD is not caused by bad parenting. But parenting techniques can often improve some symptoms and make others worse.
- Although ADHD symptoms usually continue into adulthood, the person learns ways to cope with the symptoms. People with ADHD have plenty of energy, are creative, and can often accomplish more than people who do not have the condition.
- ADHD has nothing to do with a person's intellectual ability. Some knowledgeable people have ADHD.
- Children without ADHD respond to psychostimulants similarly to children with ADHD. A trial of medicine is not used to diagnose the condition.
- Properly adjusted medicine for ADHD sharpens a person's focus and increases their ability to control behaviour.
- ADHD is estimated to affect about 3 to 7 out of 100 school-age children in the United States. footnote1 There is little evidence to support claims that ADHD is overdiagnosed and that ADHD medicines are overprescribed.
- Teens and adults with ADHD continue to benefit from medical treatment.

- ADHD is a disability. Children with ADHD have to learn ways to deal with the symptoms (inattention, impulsivity, and hyperactivity) that cause them to have difficulties in life.
- About 70 out of 100 children with ADHD continue to have symptoms during their teen years, and about 50 out of 100 have symptoms into adulthood.
- A child may not always show symptoms of ADHD, especially in an unfamiliar setting. Evaluating a child from one office observation may fail to recognize or diagnose symptoms.

CHAPTER 15: ADHD Q&A

General Questions About ADHD

What is ADHD?

Attention-deficit/hyperactivity disorder (ADHD) is a chronic neurodevelopmental disorder affecting 11 per cent of school-age children. Symptoms continue into adulthood in more than three-quarters of cases. ADHD is characterized by developmentally inappropriate levels of inattention, impulsivity, and hyperactivity.

What's The Difference Between ADD And ADHD?

In 1994, they changed the name of the disorder in a confusing way for many people. Since that time, all forms of attention deficit disorder are officially called "Attention-Deficit/Hyperactivity Disorder," regardless of whether the individual has symptoms of hyperactivity or not. Even though these are the official labels, many professionals and laypeople still use both terms: ADD and ADHD. Some use those terms to designate the old subtypes; others use ADD just as a shorter way to refer to any presentation.

How Is ADHD Diagnosed?

There is no single test to diagnose ADHD. Therefore, a comprehensive evaluation is necessary to establish a diagnosis, rule out other causes, and determine the presence or absence of coexisting conditions. Such an evaluation requires time and effort and should include a careful history and a clinical assessment of the individual's academic, social, emotional functioning and developmental level.

How Do I Find A Doctor Or Mental Health Professional?

When seeking an evaluation or treatment for ADHD, it is essential to see a qualified, licensed healthcare professional. In addition to ensuring that a particular professional has the required training, it is also necessary to work with a professional with experience dealing with this disorder.

There are several types of professionals who typically diagnose ADHD. These include physicians (especially psychiatrists, paediatricians, neurologists), psychologists, social workers, nurse practitioners, and other licensed counsellors or therapists (e.g. professional counsellors, marriage and family therapists, etc.).

Who Gets It?

ADHD affects 3 per cent to 5 per cent of all American children (approximately two million). While typically diagnosed in children, adults can also have ADHD. Adults with ADHD may be unaware they have the disorder yet know they have difficulty getting organized and staying focused. Everyday tasks such as waking up, getting dressed, arranging for the day's work, getting to work on time, or being productive on the job can be significant challenges for the ADHD adult.

What Are The Symptoms?

ADHD's principal characteristics are inattention, hyperactivity, and impulsivity. Children may exhibit one or all of these three behavioural subtypes of ADHD: predominantly hyperactive-impulsive type (without significant inattention); predominantly inattentive type (without actual hyperactive-impulsive behaviour) sometimes called ADD, an outdated term formerly used for the entire disorder; and combined type (that displays both inattentive and hyperactive-impulsive symptoms).

ADHD symptoms appear over many months, often with impulsiveness and hyperactivity preceding those of inattention. Different symptoms may occur in various settings, depending on the situation's demands for the child's self-control. Additional symptoms of ADHD may include:

- Difficulty organizing tasks and activities
- Avoids activities requiring sustained mental effort
- Loses needed items
- Forgetful of daily activities

How Is It Diagnosed?

Because symptoms may vary across settings, ADHD can be challenging to diagnose. A diagnosis of ADHD is based on the number, persistence, and history of symptomatic behaviours and the degree to which they impede a child's performance in more than one setting. Parents or teachers may be the first to notice possible signs of ADHD. Diagnosis of adult ADHD is based on symptoms, impairments, and history. Adults with ADHD might experience symptoms such as lack of focus, disorganization, restlessness, difficulty finishing projects, and losing things. They may also have problems at work, at home, or with personal relationships. Also, adults diagnosed with ADHD must have had symptoms before age seven that continued for at least six months.

Diagnosis should be made by a professional with training in ADHD or mental disorders.

Physical examinations are given to exclude such things as undetected seizures, temporal lobe seizures, and middle ear infections; psychological tests can rule out conditions such as specific learning disabilities, anxiety, or affective disorders. Ideally, reviews are made of school records, including evaluations by teachers and others about a child's behaviour based on rating scales. Parents and others who know the child well may be interviewed. Intelligence and learning tests may be administered. The specialist uses all this information to make a diagnosis of ADHD.

What Are The Causes?

ADHD is a neurological disorder, and research indicates that it may be due to alterations in the brain and the way it functions. The causes of these differences are not entirely known, but family and twin studies reveal ADHD is genetic. Between 10 per cent and

35 per cent of children with ADHD have a close relative with ADHD, and nearly half of parents who had ADHD as a child also have a child with the disorder. Studies in families of children with ADHD show that relatives are at high risk for ADHD, other psychiatric disorders, and learning disabilities.

What Are The Treatments And Side Effects?

There is no cure for ADHD and no single treatment for every child. Although ADHD is very treatable, children with the disorder seldom outgrow it. They usually develop adaptive measures to compensate for their condition. Current ADHD treatments focus on symptom management with medications and behaviour modification or with cognitive behavioural therapy.

What Other Conditions Can Occur With ADHD?

More than two-thirds of individuals with ADHD have at least one other coexisting condition. The symptoms of ADHD, constant motion and fidgetiness, interrupting and blurting out, difficulty sitting still, and the need for constant reminders, etc., may overshadow these other disorders. But just as untreated ADHD can present challenges in everyday life, other conditions can also cause unnecessary suffering in individuals with ADHD and their families if left untreated. Any infection can coexist with ADHD, but certain diseases tend to occur more commonly with ADHD. The most common conditions in ADHD are disruptive behaviour disorders, mood disorders, anxiety, tics or Tourette Syndrome, learning disorders, sleep disorders, and substance abuse.

How Is ADHD Treated?

Treating ADHD often requires medical, educational, behavioural, and psychological intervention. This comprehensive approach to treatment is sometimes called "multimodal" and, depending on the age of the individual with ADHD, may include the following:

- Parent training
- Medication
- Skills training
- Counselling
- Behavioural therapy
- Educational supports And Education regarding ADHD

What Do I Need To Know About Carrying My Medication?

Law enforcement officers pay attention to possible drug abuse, especially among teenagers and young adults. Suppose the police stop you for a traffic violation or disorderly conduct and carry ADHD medication in an unmarked container.

For Parents And Caregivers

For Adults

I'm An Adult; Doesn't ADHD Only Affect Children?

No. Approximately 10 million adults have attention-deficit/hyperactivity disorder (ADHD). About one-third of children with ADHD continue to meet the criteria for an ADHD diagnosis as adults. In early adulthood, ADHD may be associated with depression, mood or conduct disorders, and substance abuse. Adults with ADHD often cope with difficulties at work and in their personal and family lives related to ADHD symptoms. Many have inconsistent performance at work or in their careers, have problems with day-to-day responsibilities, experience relationship problems, and may have chronic feelings of frustration, guilt, or blame.

Smoking And ADHD: What's The Connection?

Research suggests that youth with ADHD are at increased risk for very early cigarette use. Cigarette smoking is more common in adolescents with ADHD, and adults with ADHD have elevated smoking rates and report particular difficulty quitting. Youth with ADHD are twice as likely to become addicted to nicotine as individuals without ADHD.

Can Someone With ADHD Join The Military?

We often receive questions from parents or teenagers who want to know whether diagnosing ADHD or taking medication to treat ADHD disqualifies someone from entering the military service. This challenge is compounded by the fact that military recruiters who have monthly recruitment quotas must meet, often giving incomplete, contradictory, or inaccurate information.

So, the simple answer to this question is...maybe.

Enlistment in the military is a multi-faceted process, and there are numerous eligibility criteria that a potential soldier, sailor, airman, or marine must meet. These criteria fall into two main categories:

- Skills and aptitude for military service
- Physical standards for military service.

These criteria are evaluated at the Military Entrance and Processing Station (MEPS) when an applicant seeks to enter the military.

Is It Safe For A Woman With ADHD To Take Stimulant Medication When Pregnant Or Plan To Become Pregnant?

The safety of stimulant medications on the developing baby during pregnancy is unknown because pregnant women are often excluded from clinical trials that study the effects of medication on them. Stimulant medications, such as amphetamines like Adderall or methylphenidates like Concerta, Ritalin LA, and Metadate CD, are all considered "Category C" medications. This means that studies of animals exposed to these medications have negatively affected their newborn pups.

Still, there are no adequate and well-controlled studies in humans to allow healthcare providers to make conclusions about the effects of these medications on human pregnancies. A Category C label also means that the benefits of using these medications during pregnancy may be acceptable despite its potential risks.

This is why all women need to talk with their doctor if they are pregnant or are planning a pregnancy and are using any medications. Together you can weigh the risks and benefits of managing your ADHD with the potential dangers of using the medicine during pregnancy.

CONCLUSION

If you think you might have ADHD, it's essential to be diagnosed by a healthcare professional. An accurate diagnosis and treatment will allow you to get relief from your symptoms and significantly improve the quality of your life. Talk to your doctor or mental health professional about the symptoms you are experiencing for a more accurate evaluation. Throughout your life and hormonal changes, be open with your doctor about your symptoms to get a clear picture of what you are experiencing when prescribing medication. Knowing that you will likely be making adjustments in treatment strategies at various stages of your life can also help you keep your ADHD symptoms under better control.

You can learn these and other new skills to help you better cope with your attention deficit disorder symptoms. Consider enrolling a trusted friend or family member, too, for additional assistance in helping to keep you on-task and more focused.

A co-occurring diagnosis of SAD can be a lifelong reality for someone with ADHD. It's OK to feel overwhelmed. Learning more about the connection between these two conditions is the first step toward lessening the impact they have on your life. Just take a deep breath and know that you can manage both ADHD and SAD with the proper support and thrive in life with the appropriate support.

Changing the way you manage your time doesn't happen overnight. Be kind to yourself and figure out what works best for you. The ideas above are just starting points. But once you take notice of how your brain works, you'll be able to figure out strategies to help you stay on track and maybe even get to your next lunch date on time. Some of the symptoms of ADHD may create difficulties in a person's sex life and romantic relationships.

The key to changing these symptoms may vary from person to person, but patience and communication between partners are crucial.

In many cases, a sex therapist or relationship counsellor with experience helping people with ADHD may provide guidance and help people with ADHD find happiness and expression in their sexual relationships. Our findings support ED symptoms as a core feature of ADHD's psychopathology. Concerning dimensions of ED, emotional lability and negative emotional responses play a more definitive role in the psychopathology of adults with ADHD. Due to insufficient statistical reports in the included studies, we could not perform meta-regression to control the function of moderator variables.

Improving your focus at work often involves a bit of experimenting and trial and error. Keep track of which strategies you're using and monitor your progress. Consider visiting a mental health professional to assist you in managing your symptoms to perform your very best.

9 781801 886185

Printed by Libri Plureos GmbH in Hamburg, Germany